# Love Stories

## of WORLD WAR II

# *Love Stories*

## *of* WORLD WAR II

### Compiled by **LARRY KING**

THREE RIVERS PRESS • NEW YORK

Published by Three Rivers Press, New York, New York.
Member of the Crown Publishing Group,
a division of Random House, Inc.
www.randomhouse.com

THREE RIVERS PRESS and the Tugboat design are registered trademarks of Random House, Inc.

All illustrations reproduced by permission of those whose stories are told, with grateful acknowledgment.

Originally published in hardcover by Crown Publishers, a division of Random House, Inc., New York, in 2001.

Printed in the United States of America

DESIGN BY BARBARA STURMAN

Library of Congress Cataloging-in-Publication Data
    Love stories of World War II / compiled by Larry King.—1st ed.
        p. cm.
    1. World War, 1939–1945—Biography.   2. Married people—
United States—Biography.   3. United States—Biography.
    I. King, Larry, 1933–   .
    D736.L68   2001
    940.53'092'2—dc21                                        2001032518

ISBN 0-609-81003-0

10   9   8   7   6   5   4   3   2   1

First Paperback Edition

*With grateful acknowledgment for the creative work of*

*John Malone and Tom Steele*

*in connection with the writing of this book.*

# CONTENTS

# $\mathscr{I}$NTRODUCTION

You are about to encounter some truly extraordinary couples, men and women who met by chance during the drama of World War II and, for the most part, stayed together for the rest of their lives. The men were going off to fight, many in legendary battles: Anzio, D-Day, the Battle of the Bulge, Guam, Iwo Jima. Some were bomber pilots or crew members flying treacherous missions over Europe and the far-flung islands of the Pacific. Others served at sea aboard destroyers, submarines, communications ships. Although many are willing to recall the battles and campaigns they lived through, altogether different stories remain more important to them. What they really like to talk about is how the war brought them together with the women who changed their lives, the women they met and loved and married in towns and cities across America, or in distant places all over the world.

Some of these couples were already in love, even married, when the United States entered World War II the day after December 7, 1941, when the Japanese bombed Pearl Harbor. But most found love in places they had never been before. Maybe a small town in the South near an army boot camp, where a girl in a red belt shone so brightly among the many pretty girls at a USO dance. Or maybe at the naval port of San Francisco, where a girl happened to emerge from a church and begin walking in the same direction as the soldier who would shortly decide he wanted to marry her. A marriage proposal might take place over the roar of air-raid sirens and pummel of anti-aircraft artillery in London. These men served in a harrowing war with diligence, courage, and distinction. But in the long run, a few intensely romantic moments changed their lives most completely—breathtaking moments when eyes met and hand brushed hand, resulting in memories to be cherished for a lifetime.

When we began gathering material for this book, we assumed that women would comprise the majority of people who wanted to tell their love stories. We were quickly disabused of that stereotypical notion. In the end, men accounted for at least half the respondents. Far from being uncomfortable with the subject of love, they relished the opportunity to tell the world about the romantic side of the World War II experience. As one man put it, "We've all got war stories. Some of us like to tell them and some don't. But the story of how we fell in love with our wives, well, that's still with us every day, and I know a lot of us can still get a little choked up over it. The war was a long time ago, one part of our lives. But we're still living the love stories. That's about now as well as then."

The wives have plenty of stories, too. You will meet a woman who decided she wasn't doing enough to help the cause by working in a defense factory, so she joined the Waves as an airplane mechanic. You will meet a spunky fifteen-year-old Neapolitan girl who was holding her sister's baby in her arms—the sister who had been killed in a bombing raid—when a GI approached to tell her that his friend was interested in her; she replied, "If he likes me so much, tell him to get some food for this baby." And you'll be introduced to women who stayed at home to care for infants whose first pictures had to be sent to a husband "somewhere" in Europe or the Pacific, a new father who might never see his child. The women's stories are as deeply felt and sometimes as dramatic as any experience their husbands might have had at the front.

Interestingly, very few of the men and women who told their stories for this book were specific about what first attracted them to the person they fell in love with. To some degree, that may be due to a generational sense of propriety. Obviously, a fervent sexual attraction between two young people must have played a large role in the initial stages of a soon-to-be-serious relationship. But nobody ever mentioned that directly. The men and women of the World War II generation still tend to believe that subtlety is worth something. Perhaps they're just true romantics in a way that is rapidly disappearing. If you ask what they think of today's movies, many of them will insist that the slightly hidden is a lot sexier than the flagrant. But perhaps it's not that they find such candor shocking; it's just that the partially veiled leaves so much, as one woman said, "to our own private dirty mind, which is much more fun."

Although these stories are told in the third person, every effort has been made to capture the voice of each teller. People were not pressed for information they did not want to give. These are *their* stories, and, in the fullest sense, this is their book. Each description of a romantic encounter contributes something special to the whole mosaic, illuminating and enlarging a broader picture of love in a time of war.

Because our cast of characters comes from such diverse backgrounds and they all had such a tremendous variety of experiences during the war, these pages enable us to see a unique period in our history from many different points of view. Though each of these stories is unique, both in circumstances and appeal, many of them reflect experiences that form common threads in the larger tapestry of World War II life. Again and again, we hear about the difficulty getting from here to there during the war years—not just overseas but right here at home. Those of us who fly a lot in this jet age, and complain endlessly about delayed flights, lousy food, and misplaced luggage, are likely to feel a little sheepish after reading these stories.

Buses, trains, planes—no matter what the mode of transportation, everyone knew there would be a problem, more likely lots of problems. Too busy making jeeps and trucks for the battlefields, Detroit had stopped making new cars. Gas was rationed, of course; you'll be hearing a lot about getting enough of it in the tank to make it through a single date, let alone connect with a loved one any distance away. Despite all the problems, luck sometimes broke the soldier's way.

Luck. A great many of the men and women whose stories appear here can still scarcely believe how lucky they were. More than one man was dismissed at the last minute from a mission on which the plane went down, killing everyone aboard. Some who did board planes that crashed ended up in the hospital for months, which would ordinarily be bad luck, except that while they were lying in bed, they first heard a nurse's voice that they would end up hearing for the rest of their lives.

Inevitably, there was horribly bad luck as well. Fifty million people died in the course of World War II, millions of civilians as well as soldiers; many survived with injuries that changed everything, including the outcome of their love stories. Not every story here has a happy ending, in the usual sense. Still, you'll see that some things are worth having even for a very short time. And sometimes what existed in the past remains so strong that years—even decades—later, it became necessary for those involved to seek out the love that was lost and try to make a new and different ending.

One of the more pleasant consequences of World War II is the fact that women from all over the world found soul mates in American men whom they might never have encountered had it not been for the war. Many international couples took enormous risks to remain together. Some parents of young women from other countries encouraged their daughters to follow their heart and embark on the highly uncertain adventure of moving to America and another way of life; other women had to overcome tremendous parental misgivings—or even sacrifice a parental relationship altogether.

The girls back home—and many of them were hardly more than that, even if they did have a newborn infant to care for—sent letters off into the unknown, to "somewhere in Europe" and "somewhere in the Pacific." They would receive letters back with blacked-out portions or even holes cut out to remove words that might threaten security. A great many of the women worried that their trivial day-to-day activities would bore their husbands and boyfriends in the midst of battle. Little did they realize they were a lifeline, helping to nourish the mind and soul of their loved ones.

Some women served away from home in the military themselves, as recruiters or nurses or airplane mechanics. Many of these women were officers, which, due to strict rules about officers of either sex fraternizing with enlisted personnel of the opposite sex, could complicate things. It took a great deal of ingenuity to get around the problem. In this book you will meet the only enlisted man actually arrested for having dinner with his wife.

Through the eyes of these men and women, you will catch sight of myriad small moments that help to convey the full panoply of a world at war: from President Franklin Delano Roosevelt's jaunty wave to a family on the streets of Hawaii as he was on his way to settle a major argument between the two most important commanders in the Pacific, to a Christmas service in the snow during the Battle of the Bulge; even the story of a German national married to an American woman who found himself incarcerated on Ellis Island with fellow "loyalty risk" Ezio Pinza, the great opera bass who was soon to become the toast of Broadway in *South Pacific*.

But above all, you'll hear the stories of "the man she was destined to marry" and "the woman across the crowded room." These love stories took place over half a century ago, but they become vivid realities once more of a time when every minute of life held a special intensity. Though this book contains many historical moments, it is not a history book. Although it demonstrates the courage of the men who fought around the world, it is not a book of war stories; it is a book of love stories. These men and women all believe that in the end, the most important facet of World War II wasn't the battles fought but the very simple fact that in the midst of war, they found each other.

# Love Stories
## of WORLD WAR II

THE BOMBING OF PEARL HARBOR on December 7, 1941, radically changed the plans of innumerable young couples across the United States practically overnight. War had been raging across Europe for over two years, ever since Adolf Hitler invaded Poland on September 1, 1939, but strong isolationist feelings dominated in the United States. President Franklin Delano Roosevelt had to muster all of his considerable cunning in order to convince Congress to institute the first peacetime draft in American history in September 1940. But with the ruthless attack on Pearl Harbor, America plunged into the war. Thousands of young couples got married over the next few months, in order to have some time together before the husband was inevitably called to duty.

*Miles and Betty Trimpey in March 1945.*

# *Miles and Betty*
## TRIMPEY

In 1998 Betty Trimpey gave her younger daughter, Linda K. Golby, a battered box of letters that had survived thirteen moves, still tied together with faded fifty-year-old hair ribbons. The letters included many that Linda's father, Miles Reid Trimpey, had written to his young wife during World War II, Betty's own letters back to him, as well as a number written to Miles by relatives and friends.

After she saw the Steven Spielberg movie *Saving Private Ryan*, Linda began wondering whether her father had been involved in the D-Day landings at Normandy. He never talked about the war before his death in 1990, and she had no idea where he served. She discovered from one letter that he indeed scrambled to the beach at Normandy that horrifying day, and spent his nineteenth birthday in a foxhole after the battle at Trévières on June 9, 1944, three days after D-Day One.

Increasingly intrigued, Linda read through all the letters and decided to type them up and assemble them in two loose-leaf volumes. She illustrated the volumes with photographs and reproductions of postcards and holiday greetings her father sent to her mother while he was in the army. She also included a number of documents pertaining to his service and annotated the top of each letter in her own elegant handwriting, explaining who had sent each letter and providing the postmark date and place. Over the following months, she also read all the letters aloud to her mother, whose eyesight had failed. The letters conjured up such vivid memories of fear and separation for Betty that the reading sessions often became extremely emotional. Linda, too, was deeply moved, as she was getting to know her father in ways she never had before.

Her father's letters were not very legible, written mostly in pencil on any paper he could get his hands on, including one on toilet tissue. Some gave the impression that a hard but not very flat surface—his helmet, his knee—was used as a writing desk. Betty maintained that she felt bad about writing her husband such boring letters, but Linda is certain that her small talk was exactly what her father needed and wanted to hear. Those letters served as his primary connection to the world he was fighting for and longed to come home to. Linda believes that the letters he sent and received actually kept him sane.

MILES TRIMPEY and Betty Romesberg both grew up near Rockwood, Pennsylvania. Betty lived with her parents on a small farm, and Miles worked in construction. They met one Saturday night when both were dining with friends at the same restaurant. Betty always told her two daughters, Nancy Lee and Linda, that it was love at first sight, and Miles would say that he had thought Betty was the most beautiful girl he'd ever seen in his life and that he knew instantly that he would marry her someday.

On their first date, Miles took Betty to the construction site where he was working, to show her that he was a hardworking, serious young man. In fact, he was only seventeen, and Betty eighteen. They soon married, on April 14, 1943. Because Miles expected to be drafted shortly after he turned eighteen, they moved in with Betty's parents instead of trying to find their own place. They also decided to have a baby right away. Miles wanted to have at least one child in case he didn't make it home from the war, and Betty agreed.

On June 9, 1943, Miles turned eighteen, and sure enough, the notice to report for induction (Order #12,472) was issued on September 13. He became an enlisted man on October 19 and was sent to Camp Wheeler, Georgia, for basic training. As soon as he got to camp, he started writing the letters that Betty prized so much.

In a letter from Camp Wheeler dated October 22, Miles told Betty that they had watched a movie show at the camp. "They were no good," he wrote, "but if I had you with me they would be better." On October

28, he noted, "I had to stop this letter just now. We were called out for a little training. We had to learn to salute an officer."

Training quickly got serious. In a November 4 letter, Miles told Betty that he had bought her a souvenir, a miniature replica of the automatic rifle he had been trained to use: "It shoots eight shells as fast as you can pull the trigger. Take notice of the knife on the end. They showed us how to kill a man with it today. You use the knife if you don't have any shells. The knife is 16" long. You run it through the neck or through the guts."

As if realizing that this description might upset Betty, he started a new paragraph: "To change the subject I want to thank you for the Bible you sent me. I will use it and often." Betty still has that small blue Bible, a bit tattered from its wartime service. On the flyleaf he inscribed his name, rank, and serial number, and listed Mrs. Miles Trimpey, Rockwood, Pa, R.D. #1, Box 6, as his nearest relative. On the opposite page was a printed note from the White House: "As Commander-in-Chief I take pleasure in commending the reading of the Bible to all who serve in the armed forces of the United States," it begins, and it is signed Franklin D. Roosevelt. It is clear from Miles's letters that he did use that Bible often and, like many others, learned to pray with considerably more urgency while serving in the war. As for the souvenir gun, Betty wrote to tell him that it was beautiful, and that she had placed it on her bureau as he had asked.

As the seventeen weeks of training continued, Miles wrote as often as possible, practically daily, but sometimes he was too exhausted to do anything but collapse at the end of the day. His letters are suffused with love for Betty and his concern about how she was feeling as her pregnancy advanced. (The word "pregnant" was not used by either of them; Betty spoke instead of "my condition," as proper young women were taught to do sixty years ago.)

There was discussion of Betty coming down to Georgia to see Miles, because he would not be able to come home for Thanksgiving or Christmas, but both finances and her "condition" prevented that. Miles did not get his first pay, which, after the allotment sent home to Betty was $15 for the month he had served, until November 30, and it was thanks only to dollar bills sent by relatives that he was able to buy much of anything. Betty and other family members and friends also sent him treats like candy and nuts. At one point he asked Betty to send him some "cigs," and more than once he wryly noted, "Another day, another 60 cents." When he did get paid, he went out and had his picture taken in uniform to send to Betty. It arrived with the frame and glass broken, despite his careful wrapping. In response, Betty offered some wifely advice about marking any other pictures "Glass, Handle with Care" or, even better, sending just the photo marked "Picture, Do Not Bend" and letting her buy a frame. But even with a broken frame, she loved the photo and wrote to him, "Boy are you ever good-looking."

When the couple exchanged Christmas letters, Betty wrote that it surely didn't feel like Christmas without him. After describing the family feast, she commented, "I wasn't very hungry for any food. All I was hungry for is your love." Miles described his meal, including turkey and pumpkin pie and "most everything we could think of," adding, "The only time you get a good meal in the Army is Thanksgiving or Christmas." He closed by telling her, "I hear 'White Christmas' playing. Does it ever bring back the good old days. I feel like crying. No fooling. Your True Husband, Miles."

Army realities soon returned to the foreground. In a letter written on the twenty-ninth, Miles complained, "We got a new sergeant yesterday and is he ever hell on earth." It was already clear that he would be "going over," using the phrase for European combat that was initiated during World War I. For a while, Miles had written about trying to join the paratroopers, but when he asked Betty what she thought, she firmly discouraged the idea, since his situation was likely to be dangerous enough without any leaping out of planes.

Like all soldiers, Miles was well aware that he could easily get killed. In his Christmas Day letter, he wrote, "So, Darling, never worry if anything happens to me and I never get back. Always think of these words, 'I will be in Heaven waiting for you, Darling.'" But however much he may have worried about what could happen to him, other letters make clear his pride in being a good soldier, and his delight that his unit had been singled out by an officer as the best around.

As his training drew to a grueling close, Miles had to spend two weeks living in a tent in the woods while his unit was put through combat exercises. Despite the cold and rain and lack of sleep, he was sustained by the hope that at the end of his training, he would get a week's leave to go north and be with Betty. The leave he prayed for came through at the end of February, and he was able to spend the first week of March with his wife, by then seven months "on the way." They shared an all too brief, bittersweet interlude, knowing every moment that Miles was about to be shipped overseas into battle.

On March 7, 1944, Miles was at Fort George G. Meade in Maryland, writing home "to my one I love most in all the world." The next day he was furnished with all new equipment for his overseas posting—where, exactly, he still didn't know.

On the thirteenth he received his shipping orders and wrote to Betty telling her not to worry if at any time she didn't hear from him for a couple of weeks. He sent her a cross and told her that while it might not cost much, "if you just think of it and the fellow who got it for you, I know it will help me get back much sooner and in good health." He promised to read his little blue Bible: "I know if I read it and live up to what it says, I will be back to you. And Darling you do the same. Darling, I wish I could hand you this letter . . . like a little baby with tears in my eyes I have to quit."

On the fourteenth, Miles wrote twice and must have tried to give her some hint about where he was being sent, since sections of the letter were blacked out by censors. There was one more letter from Maryland, and then two with no postmark. The next one came by V-Mail, written April 7 but postmarked April 18. Miles Trimpey was now overseas.

Miles added some new words to the flyleaf of his Bible during the transatlantic crossing: "April 2, 1944. As I lie here on this boat thinking how much I love you, I will give my life for you or the baby." He sent short notes by V-Mail for more than a month before he finally heard back that their baby daughter, Nancy Lee, had been born on April 30, 1944. "The best news I ever had in my whole life," Miles wrote in a letter dated May 12 but postmarked June 9—two days after D-Day, as he celebrated his nineteenth birthday in a cold, wet foxhole. Miles did not actually find out the baby's name until May 25, but from then on, his letters were usually addressed to both Betty and Nancy Lee. The letters Betty sent to him during this period were lost, but the first tangible evidence of his daughter survived: Betty sent him a piece of paper with Nancy Lee's inked footprints on it, and he put it in his Bible for safekeeping.

By the end of June, Miles was able to write "Somewhere in France" at the top of his letters. On July 4 he wrote about having gone to church the day before with other GIs and told Betty she should have seen how they all prayed and sang. "I believe this war made a lot of fellows look hard at their homes and wives and country and see how good they had it. I believe this war is to make people think a little more of God and to go to church a little more instead of going to a beer party. . . . Lots of people back home in the states still don't care, but I know for myself and the boys who've been on the battlefield and saw fighting do care. It made them all think . . . about living a different life." This was the letter written on toilet paper.

Over the following three months, the letters from Miles were short and intermittent. He seldom complained, and the roar of the war came through only once in a while, as when he reported seeing an American plane shot out of the sky but noticed figures parachuting from it and so assumed they were safe. He wrote about his respect for the Army Air Force, and about how much they had done to speed the way of American troops across France. He told of three soldiers praying in a foxhole and revealed that he was one of them. Always, he wrote longingly about his daughter and how he and Betty would raise her to be a good girl when he got home.

On October 1, 1944, he excitedly wrote: "Well, Darling, I am in Paris. I never thought a year ago I would be in Paris." He had finally received a picture of little Nancy Lee, and he declared her very cute, adding, "I never knew I was man enough. Ha, Ha."

Later in the month he referred to the Parisian postcards he had sent home, noting that now he had seen all those places. "Boy, this is too pretty of a country for a war," he added, echoing the thoughts of so many American soldiers who fought their way across historic lands they had never expected to see.

On November 15 he was somewhere in Belgium. Two days later he wrote, "You know a man never knows what a wife and a home means until he goes to the other side of the world. And, Darling, I am in Germany now."

On the twentieth, he forwarded home a poem, author unknown, that celebrated his regiment, "The Thirty Eighth (The Rock of the Marne)." The poem closes:

> In Conclusion, When Our Work Is Done
> Then Read of the Battles One By One
> For Our Part to You Folks at Home It Will Be
> "You're Welcome!"
> FROM THE 38TH INFANTRY.

There was one more brief letter, written on Thanksgiving Day, then Miles was separated from the Thirty-eighth, wounded in action.

A letter from the War Department, dated December 26, 1944, informed Betty Trimpey, "the latest report from the theater of operations states that on 9 December the recovery of your husband, Private Miles R. Trimpey, was not proceeding satisfactorily." The letter went on to tell her that some of America's finest doctors were assigned to overseas bases and that her husband was receiving the very best of medical care. At home in Pennsylvania, Betty could only wait helplessly for more news. It was not until January 11 that a two-week-old letter arrived to announce that Miles was "convalescing" and that further news would come as soon as possible.

Betty wrote to the War Department to beseech them for any information they could possibly give her and received a reply dated February 6: "Neither the original report showing that he was seriously wounded in action on 24 November, 1944, nor the progress reports reveal the nature and extent of his wounds. . . . With respect to your inquiry regarding the whereabouts of your husband, you will undoubtedly realize that in the interest of military security his present location cannot be disclosed."

Fortunately, a document bearing the previous day's date arrived, bringing far better news. It was from Thomas M. England General Hospital in Atlantic City, New Jersey, with Miles's name and serial number typed in, along with a description of his condition as "satisfactory." Best of all, the notice informed Betty that "You may visit him if you desire," and gave visiting hours.

There was also a letter from Miles, the first in two and a half months, dated February 7 and postmarked the same day in Atlantic City. "To the one I love most and will be seeing soon," it began, then continued: "Well,

*Miles Trimpey in 1944.*

THE WHITE HOUSE
WASHINGTON

As Commander-in-Chief I take pleasure in commending the reading of the Bible to all who serve in the armed forces of the United States. Throughout the centuries men of many faiths and diverse origins have found in the Sacred Book words of wisdom, counsel and inspiration. It is a fountain of strength and now, as always, an aid in attaining the highest aspirations of the human soul.

*The Bible that Betty sent to Miles, with his note: "As I lie here on this boat thinking how much I love you, I will give my life for you or the baby."*

*Here is your daughter Nancy Lee's footprints.*

*Put this in your Bible and keep it with you with lots of love.*

*V....*

The paper with baby
Nancy Lee's footprints.

Miles and Nancy Lee
Trimpey in June 1945.

honey, I guess our prayers were answered. I had to get shot a few times to get back but I am here now."

Although Betty and Miles were able to see each other often, it was not until mid-July that his convalescence was completed and he received his discharge papers. Just before he returned home for good, he wrote a letter from the hospital on July 17 telling Betty that he had received two books from his old division the day before. "I will give you one and Mom one. They tell of every battle I have been in and every country and how many men were killed and wounded. We had 5,020 men killed and wounded. Quite a few. So I will close now. And write, Love Always, Your Old Man, Miles."

WHEN AMERICA ENTERED THE war, many young couples were already engaged, so they simply moved up their wedding date. But for many others, the war created more complicated circumstances. Some decided to delay marriage, usually because the man felt it was unfair to go off to war and leave behind a bride he might never see again. For still others, the advent of war gave a new relationship a sudden ardency. A wedding that might not have taken place for another year or longer now seemed a matter of urgency. Proposals were offered and quickly accepted. But even if both people wanted a hasty marriage, they usually faced obstacles. One way around such problems was to elope.

*Doris and William Metzger in September 1943.*

# *William and Doris*

## METZGER

William Metzger, Jr., was born in Philadelphia, Pennsylvania, but his family soon relocated to Atlantic City, New Jersey. He met his future wife, Doris, there—although, as they fondly recall, she was not much taken with him initially. Bill was, he admits, a bit rowdy and rough around the edges. He rode a motorcycle and was a daredevil driver. After his second accident, a prankster at the Atlantic City hotel where he worked secretly put a sticker that said "Wild Bill" on the windshield of his bike.

But Bill eventually won Doris over, and their relationship had grown quite serious by the time Pearl Harbor was bombed on December 7, 1941. He had a low number in the draft and knew he would soon be called up for duty. But he'd always wanted to learn to fly, so he persuaded his draft board to delay his date for a couple of months while he attended ground school.

While attending the school, he kept seeing a guy he didn't know, seeming to watch him from the sidelines. Bill finally asked an instructor who it was. The instructor told him that the man was from the draft board and was keeping an eye on Bill to make certain he was really learning to fly and not just dodging the draft.

Bill got into the air and began flying Piper Cubs. After his last night of classes, he dropped by Doris's house, and they discussed the likelihood of his being drafted any day. They were both Catholics, and in those days the Church didn't allow weddings during Lent, which had just begun.

Chances seemed all too likely that he would be gone by Easter, some forty days later. Doris agreed they should get married right away, and they decided to take a quick trip down to Maryland, where no waiting period was necessary. The weather was bad, and a trip on his motorcycle in the rain seemed out of the question. So on March 9, 1942, they borrowed Doris's parents' car and left a note saying simply, "We have gone to get married. Please don't worry. Wish us luck." Because Bill didn't have much money at the time, he bought Doris a $22 wedding band but didn't have any extra money for his own band. Instead, he took the signet right he was wearing and turned it so that just the band showed on the top of his finger and told her that would be his wedding ring. He's been wearing the ring that way ever since, for the fifty-nine years of their marriage.

When Doris and Bill returned home to "face the music," they were told that they needn't have eloped after all. Unbeknownst to them, the Church had made a special dispensation for weddings during Lent because so many young men were being drafted. So on April 6 they were married again in church, giving them two anniversaries to celebrate. As Bill recalls with humor, when he left work one day not long after he and Doris were married, he found a new message written on his motorcycle windshield: "Wild Bill Is Sweet William Now."

With his flying-school experience putting him in good stead, Bill was accepted into the army air corps. Although his pay was only $90 a month, Doris managed to stay with him throughout his training period, which involved several moves, starting out at Maxwell Field in Montgomery, Alabama, for preflight training, and then to several different fields in Georgia, Mississippi, and Arkansas, where he graduated and received his wings. He was then sent to El Paso, Texas, for postflight training on B-24s. There were only a few wives living off-base in El Paso, and while life was certainly not easy for them, sometimes Bill and his friends managed to smuggle out food to help them stretch their meager budgets. Bill was confined to base during the week but had a day pass on Saturdays. Doris got to know all the young men with whom he was in training, and a group of them tooled off one time to Juarez, Mexico, for some Saturday-night carousing.

After El Paso, Bill was sent to Harrington, Kansas, for his plane assignment. As soon as Bill saw the plane, he knew he was heading to the North African desert rather than the European campaign: The plane was pink, the camouflage color used in North Africa.

During World War II, it was common practice for a crew to give their plane a name, and they often painted a picture on the nose cone to further distinguish themselves. The pilot—in this case Bill—usually got to choose the name, but Doris said that wasn't fair, and she suggested that everyone put a name on a slip of paper to be drawn out of a hat. That meant there could be as many as ten different possible names, one for each member of the crew. But that wasn't how it worked out.

The crew members had gotten to know one another quite well by this time through off-hours socializing, and they all remembered a story Doris had told them about the tragic death of Bill's sister's young son Jackie, always called Jackie Boy. He had been quite a lively, unruly child, always getting into minor scrapes. On one occasion, he tried to hitch a ride on the back of a horse-drawn milk truck in his neighborhood and managed to pull a box of empty glass milk bottles onto his head. Bill's sister had stayed in Atlantic City near their family when she married. She lived on the bank of the inlet spilling into the bay, and the neighborhood kids regularly climbed the fence behind the houses—meant to keep them from the water—to go fishing. One day Jackie Boy fell from the fence and drowned. His own father discovered the body as he was walking home from work later that day. Everyone in Bill's crew had been touched by the story, and every single slip of paper selected from the hat said the same thing: "Jackie Boy."

A picture was painted on the plane's nose of a little boy with a dog at his feet and angel wings sprouting from his shoulders. Then the *Jackie Boy* flew off to combat in North Africa, separating Doris and Bill for the first time. She returned to Atlantic City to live with her parents for the duration of the war.

Bill and his crew flew missions to Europe out of Libya and then Tunisia, and were then dispatched up to Italy when the American invasion began in the fall of 1943. By early December they were flying missions out of Italy over Greece, which the Nazis had invaded and still largely controlled though by this time a civil war had also broken out.

Fortunately for the crew of the *Jackie Boy*, Greece was the home of an estimable British underground operation, as well as a growing Greek underground.

On December 6, Bill's plane was running a bombing mission over Athens when it was hit hard by German ground fire. The plane's windshield was shattered, and both Bill and his copilot were injured: Bill was shot and a piece of one of his ears was nicked off. When Bill surveyed the damage to the plane, he quickly realized they were in grave danger: the number-one engine was smoking and the number-two engine was fully ablaze. Bill feathered the number-three engine, meaning he turned its blades in such a way that it would create less drag on the airplane. Bill had little control over the plane, which was definitely going down. The only question was how far from German troops they could get. Bill fought hard to keep the plane aloft long enough to get away from Athens, which he says was "crawling with Germans," and headed out toward the surrounding hills. When he felt he could hold the plane no longer, he gave the call to bail out. The bombardier and navigator jumped out through the wheel hatch under the nose of the plane. The rest of the crew jumped out from the rear. Bill and his copilot were the last left. They could see German army trucks on a road below them.

The copilot had volunteered to substitute for the crew's regular copilot, who was sick. Not being assigned to a regular crew, he chose to fly with a flight crew he knew and trusted rather than being sent on a flight with "some hammerhead" pilot, as Bill says. He picked the right man to fly with that day.

As Bill prepared to bail out, he noticed the copilot struggling with his parachute, which was the bulky seat-pack style as opposed to the chest-pack style Bill wore. The seat-pack parachutes made maneuvering in the cockpit difficult, and the copilot was having a hard time getting himself free. Bill stopped to help him, and they both managed to eject and descend safely.

Once on the ground, Bill and the five crew members nearby faced the new danger of capture by German troops. They started running up the side of a mountain, looking to find cover, and saw a farm field up ahead. Then they spotted a young boy in the field waving his hands toward them, motioning to them to go back the way they'd come, or so they thought. They expected he was warning them away from German troops. Later, once they'd made their way to safety, they learned that in Greece that gesture means to come forward. They also discovered later that three of the crew had been less fortunate and were captured by the Germans. One of them was injured upon landing, and the others were slowed by stopping to help him.

Thanks to the British and Greek underground, Bill and five of his crew managed to get out of Greece by various routes. Bill and the copilot were smuggled out of the country by boat to Turkey. They were provided with false papers and civilian clothes, which were mysteriously pitched in through their hotel-room door by someone they never saw. First they had to make their way to Zelos in northern Greece, and from there they caught a boat that delivered them into Allied hands in Turkey. They made their escape on Christmas Day. On New Year's Day, they took a train south into Syria. From there, a British army officer arranged for them to fly to Cairo, where there was an Allied base. They arrived "looking like a bunch of bums," as Bill recalls. From Cairo, Bill sent Doris a cryptic telegram, selecting his message from a limited list of phrases approved by the military for use in telegrams: "All well. Children return home."

Back home in Atlantic City, Doris had received a telegram from the War Department on New Year's Day, informing her that Bill's plane had been shot down over enemy territory and that he was missing in action. She took the news calmly at first, but when she went over to her in-laws' house to tell them the news, she suddenly fainted and hit her head so hard on a radiator that she knocked herself out. The next day, Doris received a letter from a Lieutenant William Ashburn, who had been flying with Bill's squadron and had seen the plane go down. He reported that "it couldn't have happened in a better place," because many soldiers had been able to escape from that area; he had seen all of the crew "hit the silk," the colorful phrase used at the time for bailing out, and none of them had "hit the drink." Doris then wrote letters to the families of the other crew members to give them this good word.

After the ordeal he'd been through, Bill was reassigned to the States to train other fliers. He received the Purple Heart, and that wasn't the only medal he received for actions under fire, although he didn't know about the other until years later. Bill liked flying so much that he decided to stay in the army after the war, and one day in 1951, on a whim, he and a friend went to headquarters to look up their service records. There was the record of the Purple Heart and several other medals, as well as one he didn't recognize.

"What does 'SS' mean?" he asked the secretary in the office.

"Silver Star," she replied. "You got the Silver Star."

"First I've heard of it," Bill exclaimed.

The prestigious medal had been awarded to him in 1943, but he was never notified, which was not an uncommon occurrence in World War II. He had received it for keeping his plane in the air long enough to allow most of his crew to jump to safety.

During his postwar years in the army, Bill served as an instructor in a number of locations, including Nashville, Tennessee; Charleston, South Carolina; and locations around Texas and Florida. Although the moving around could be difficult at times, Doris insists it was nothing like the days when they were first married, when they had to move every nine weeks as Bill's training progressed, and they were often practically starving.

In 1953 Bill was "fired by Ike," as the soldiers of that period ironically referred to the downsizing of the military after Eisenhower became president and ended the Korean War. Bill was stationed at Westover, Massachusetts, at the time, and he and Doris had to decide whether to stay in that area and look for work, or return with their son and two daughters to their home grounds of Atlantic City. As it happened, the bombardier from the *Jackie Boy* had left the army right after the war and opened a successful clothing business in northwestern Massachusetts. He wanted to open a branch business in Northampton, the home of Smith College, and was looking for someone he completely trusted to run the branch. He offered the job to Bill.

The family was glad to stay. Not only is Northampton a beautiful part of the country, the daughters of residents could attend Smith for free—if they could do the academic work—which one of their daughters took advantage of.

*Doris with Bill after the 1943 ceremony during which he graduated and received his wings.*

A Valentine's Day card that Bill
sent Doris, on which he wrote,
"Roses are red, violets are blue,
the bees love honey, and I love you."
With a special note: "Junior is in the middle."

The note that Doris and Bill left for her parents before borrowing the car to go
and get married.

Bill and Doris while waiting for Sunday dinner, which cost $1.60 for two, at Mrs. Ketchem's Boarding House in Americus, Georgia. They saved all week.

Bill and Doris having fun in Juarez, Mexico, in 1943.

Today, Bill and Doris Metzger still live in Northampton and have nine grandchildren and four great-grandchildren. At the age of eighty-four, Bill works out six days a week. When he tells the story of being shot down over Greece, Doris makes sure he adds that she knocked herself out on that radiator on New Year's Day in 1944, when she got the news that her husband was missing.

M ANY YOUNG MEN AND WOMEN already had sweethearts when America entered the war, but at least as many others were still looking for that special person to settle down with. Unattached young men left their hometowns for training bases all over the United States. Some young women did the same thing. They weren't looking for romance, they were fighting a war, but in their new surroundings, some of these young people met in chance encounters that led to a whole life together.

*Earl and Maxine Butterfield shortly after
they were married in 1947.*

# *Earl and Maxine*
## BUTTERFIELD

In the summer of 1943, Second Lieutenant Earl Butterfield was busy assembling a B-24 bomber crew in Boise, Idaho, and training them for duty. One evening after going out in the town near the base, Earl boarded the bus back. "It was crowded with servicemen returning to base and civilians going to work on the graveyard shift," Earl recalls. "The driver made a very sudden stop, and all the people standing were thrown forward. I grabbed a girl in coveralls to keep her from hitting the windshield. She thanked me and told me she was working as an aircraft electrician. Before we could say much more, we arrived at the base. She intrigued me, and I boarded the same bus a couple of more times, hoping to see her, but I didn't."

Then one Saturday night not long after, when Earl was waiting to cross a street in Boise, two girls happened to drive by. One of them was the girl from the bus, and she and Earl recognized each other immediately. Moments later, the two girls walked up to Earl. They told him they were going bowling, and Earl asked if he could join them.

He discovered that the girls were roommates, and that they had worked for only a few days at the base in Boise en route from Everett, Washington, to a base near Boise in Mountain Home, Idaho. They hadn't been able to find a decent place to live at the new base, so they were commuting from Boise. The name of the girl Earl met on the bus was Maxine Cole.

After that night, Earl and Maxine went on a couple of dates, but suddenly he was transferred to another base, and after that to the Southwest Pacific. "I wrote to Maxine from the Pacific, as well as to several other girls," Earl explains, "including another one from Boise whom I had dated several times. Maxine wrote the most interesting letters, although they were quite . . . platonic."

When it appeared that he would make it back to the States in the spring of 1945, Earl wrote first to Margery, the other girl in Boise, asking her to meet him in Salt Lake City as he traveled by train across the country to his home in Syracuse, New York. After a few weeks, when he hadn't heard back from Margery, he wrote to Maxine and asked if *she* would meet him. When Maxine told her boss, who was a woman, about getting invited to Salt Lake by a guy she hardly knew, her boss asked what his rank was. "When Maxine said I was a captain," Earl recalls, "her boss said I would be loaded with money, and promptly wrote out leave papers so Maxine could go help me spend it."

When Earl arrived in San Francisco that April, he wired a hotel in Salt Lake City right away to make a reservation for two rooms. Getting no reply, he assumed they were set. "Wartime trains were notoriously late, and mine was no exception. Somewhere along the line, I wired Maxine that I would be late, but she never received the telegram. By the time I caught up with her, she was ready to turn around and go back to Boise. After a long-delayed dinner, we had to start searching for rooms, as my reservation was not honored. But we spent about three days in Salt Lake and got much better acquainted."

Earl and Maxine continued to correspond, with increasing ardor. He left the service and returned to his old job in Buffalo, New York, while she remained in Boise. Then, in the summer of 1946, Maxine and her girlfriend Lillian went east, Lillian to visit her fiancé in Oil City, Pennsylvania, and Maxine to see Earl. Earl took some time off to take Maxine to Syracuse to meet his parents. Then she went back to Boise, and many more letters were exchanged.

At the end of the year, Maxine invited Earl to Boise for a New Year's celebration, but she didn't think he'd come all that way, so she accepted another date. She was completely flabbergasted when Earl notified her that he'd be there, and she had to beg off the other date.

When Earl arrived, Maxine told him she'd just lost her job at the Idaho statehouse; the new Republican administration had replaced all the political appointees.

"Her brother Bob loaned us his Oldsmobile," Earl explained, "so we had wheels to explore the area. After seeing about everything we wanted to see, we began to explore our relationship. One fine sunny day, I facetiously said that if it weren't such a bureaucratic hassle, it would be a good day to get married. Maxine quickly replied that she could smooth the way because she knew everyone at the statehouse, and they'd process our application without delay."

They took blood tests that very day and picked up their license at the Idaho capital the day after. Earl and Maxine were married in the Methodist parsonage by Dr. Forrest Werts on January 9, 1947. Maxine's friend Lillian was her attendant, and a fellow pilot from Earl's home area, who happened to be living in Boise at the time, served as best man. After a small reception with Maxine's friends and relatives, the couple honeymooned in McCall, Idaho, thanks to her brother's Oldsmobile.

Earl and Maxine raised two children, and now they have two grandchildren. They're still together after fifty-four years, and it's all because a bus driver slammed on the brakes.

*Earl Butterfield as a second lieutenant at Gowen Field in Boise, Idaho, in 1943.*

*Earl Butterfield's crew (Earl is in the center of the back row) in New Guinea in 1944.*

*Earl and Maxine on their fiftieth wedding anniversary.*

W HEN HOMETOWN SWEETHEARTS were separated by the war, communication became a serious issue. Mail was sluggish, even within the United States. Letters sent from North Africa or the European theater could take weeks to find their way home, and those dispatched from the South Pacific usually took even longer. Mail often arrived in bunches, both at the fronts and back home. The letters from home helped keep the fighting men sane, while those sent back assured that a loved one was still safe—at least as of a few weeks earlier. All letters were treasured, but some were particularly special: Some servicemen employed special talents to enliven their messages.

*Ed and Mary Jane Russell shortly after they were married.*

# *Ed and Mary Jane*
## RUSSELL

During his last year of high school in Teaneck, New Jersey, Ed Russell drew a comic strip for the school paper. His main character was "Itchie," a skinny guy with big clown eyes and a prominent red nose. Ed recalls, "That same year"—1943—"I was introduced to the prettiest, smartest, and most popular young lady in school, if not in the entire United States of America. She said to me, 'I know you. You draw those wonderful cartoons.' I replied, 'For that I'm going to marry you.'" The name of the young lady who liked his cartoons was Mary Jane Walton. They went on just one date before he joined the navy. Ed remembers knowing that he would "have to work very hard" if he was going to realize his marital intentions.

In early May 1943, five weeks before graduation, Ed left for boot camp. The navy had not been his first choice. He and his friend Billy Roauer fervently wanted to join the marines, but they were underweight. As things turned out, Ed was assigned to duty with the marines after all.

After completing radio school at the University of Chicago, where he learned to send and receive Morse code, Ed was sent for training at the Marine Communications School, Amphibious Training, Pacific, at Port Hueneme, California. "We were issued marine combat gear and trained to set up and operate portable radios and portable generators," he says now. "Both pieces of equipment were very heavy. They were carried on our backs, which would make it very difficult to find a place to hide when in combat. Not to worry, we were told. The Japanese would probably mistake the radios for the dreaded flamethrowers"—weapons that shot streams of napalm, a jelly-like petroleum mixture that sticks to the skin and burns. They were used to devastating effect by the U.S. forces in the Pacific campaign.

While at Port Hueneme, Ed also took crash courses in amphibious landings and hand-to-hand combat, and he realized that the Morse code he had learned in Chicago wasn't going to count for much in the job he was now being prepared for. He underwent still further training at the marine base at Camp Pendleton, near Oceanside, California. Spending all that time as a navy man training alongside marines, Ed now notes wryly, "made it clear that sailors and marines didn't always get along."

Right from the beginning of training, Ed sent letters to Mary Jane in Teaneck, and these letters looked like no others sent to sweethearts back home. The envelopes were decorated with irresistibly charming cartoons featuring his character Itchie. An early one from Camp Pendleton displayed Itchie as the grinning pilot of a navy dive-bomber, with a sailor hat perched atop his virtually shaved head, trailing a "Via Air Mail" banner behind his plane. In one hand Itchie held a letter bearing Mary Jane's address, placed just perfectly so that the stamp on Ed's drawn letter was the real six-cent U.S. airmail stamp. On another envelope, Itchie morphed into a wryly smiling seaplane, with big eyes and nose serving as the plane's windshield and nose turret, a sailor hat perched between the wings. In the letter itself, Ed wrote, "Sometimes this love business can be regular hell. That's only when there's half the world between us, definitely not when we will be together. Yes, I love you Miss Walton."

These enchanting envelopes soon winged their way to Mary Jane from the South Pacific, where Ed was assigned to duty, reaching her at a summer vacation job, then at Sarah Lawrence College, as well as at her family home back in Teaneck. Ed also sent Itchie letters to his mother and—no fool he—to Mary Jane's mother.

Although Ed tried hard to be upbeat, using Itchie to raise his own spirits as well as those of Mary Jane and others back home, his service in the Pacific was often quite dangerous. He served aboard the U.S.S. *Hamlin* when she arrived at Iwo Jima less than twenty-four hours after the first wave of marines hit the shore on February 19, 1945. The ship was anchored near what the sailors and marines nicknamed "Hot Rock": Mount Suribachi, on which, as captured in one of the most celebrated photographs of World War II, the marines raised the American flag on February 23.

Ed recalls watching the battle of Iwo Jima from his ship: "We had front-row seats to the bloodiest battle of the war. Tank duels, aerial strafing attacks, and the two flag-raisings all took place within a few hundred yards of our ship. During one air raid, several of us went topside to watch. Anti-aircraft fire was so thick it had to be witnessed to be believed. Suddenly my buddy Pete Rooney yelled, 'I'm hit!' We ducked inside; his wound was a tiny piece of hot shrapnel in his palm. The next day we gave him a 'Purple Palm' as a thank-you for scaring us so. A few days later, the *Hamlin* was hit in the stack by a mortar shell while I was on radio watch just twenty feet away. Fortunately, the shell was a dud. Watching that battle made me glad I was not a marine."

But Ed's most harrowing experience of the war took place on the U.S.S. *Curtiss.* On June 21, 1945, the ship was the target of a savage kamikaze attack. "It started at twilight," he recalls. "Pete Rooney, Doc Savage, and I were on the fantail playing cards. An announcement had just come over the PA system telling us organized resistance on Okinawa had ended. The area was 'secure.' I noticed two fighters off in the distance doing loops. Unusual. I realized they were Japanese and let out a yell. No general quarters had been sounded. Also unusual." The Japanese planes were sending out a high-frequency radio signal that American planes transmitted to let Allied radar operators know they were friendly. The Japanese had cleverly transferred two of the signal devices from downed American planes to their own aircraft. "Their code signal was wrong," Ed says, "but radar did not report them as 'bogeys' because such an error was common."

One of the Japanese fighters, code-named Frank, "dove straight down, pulled out, and headed for my nose. Actually, he headed for my shoelaces; the deck I was on was thirty feet above the waterline, and he was below it. Those around me scattered. I stood and watched, amazed at what he was doing. He flew so low his propeller stirred up a wake in the water. I said, 'How can you do it?' and stayed with him all the way. I have no recollection of being frightened. When he got very close, he dipped one wingtip into the water, driving the plane amidship. He hit the photo lab and the sick bay, right above bomb storage. We had just taken aboard a batch of aerial torpedoes, and when they got the fire out fifteen and a half hours later, the torpedoes were just a mass of twisted metal. It was a miracle we weren't blown to kingdom come. We suffered sixty-one casualties, including thirty-seven killed."

After months of grueling service in these last battles of the Pacific campaign, the war was finally over. Ed received word that he would soon be heading home. He had been away from home, and from Mary Jane, for more than two years. Of course Mary Jane was alerted to his return by a special message from Itchie. In this letter, Itchie was perched on a graceful curve identified as "MJ's knee." The message below read:

"DEAR MARY JANE. This is Itchie talking, and we've got a serious problem. Eddie is coming home, and you have fallen in love with me.

What are we going to do about Eddie?

Beginning at the beginning, how are you going to greet him? Shake hands? Kiss? If so, will it be a kiss on the cheek? Or will it be an explosive release of suppressed passion you have held back for the last 28 months?

I suggest you go all out.

Ed had written to Mary Jane from the Pacific that he was ready to marry her; when she was ready, all she had to do was ask. Not long after he returned home in January 1946, she said she was ready, though her college schedule and a summer job precluded a wedding until the following December. Ed suggested December 21 because it is the longest night of the year, and Mary Jane agreed because it fell on a Saturday, which was a good day for a wedding.

Both Edward T. Russell and Mary Jane Walton Russell went on to make great use of their natural talents. Ed took a job in advertising and in seventeen years rose to become president of the legendary agency Doyle Dane Bernbach International. With her startling good looks, Mary Jane became a successful high-fashion model. One of her many magazine covers was the famous "Beauty Issue" of *Harper's Bazaar* for April 1953, during the glory days of high-fashion photography. Mary Jane appeared

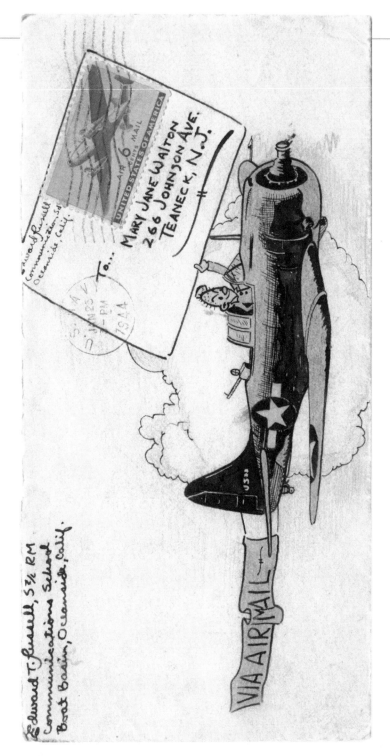

*Itchie as a pilot, delivering a letter to Mary Jane from the amphibious training school at Camp Pendleton, California.*

*Itchie, morphed into a plane.*

Itchie sitting on Mary Jane's knee. Away for over two years, Ed realized Mary Jane might have another boyfriend. He wrote this letter when he was on his way home.

*Iwo Jima's Mount Suribachi, photographed from the seaplane tender U.S.S. Hamlin on February 24, the day after the famous flag-raising. The flag can be seen (circled), near the top right crest. (Photo courtesy of Fred Munkner)*

*Above: Ed and Mary Jane Russell in black tie, posing for a photo shoot with famed photographer Louise Dahl-Wolfe during Mary Jane's modeling career. Right: Mary Jane on the cover of the April 1953* Harper's Bazaar.

in profile, wearing a large-brimmed chartreuse hat with a huge bow at the back, holding two black lacquered palm-shaped fans at right angles. She looked almost untouchably elegant. But of course the real Mary Jane fell in love with a scamp of a cartoon character named Itchie—not to mention his creator.

I F THE LOVE LETTERS THAT TRAVERSED *the world during the war kept hope alive for the soldiers and their loved ones back home, a package could provide a special, more tangible kind of solace. Not only did soldiers receive packages from home, many soldiers also sent home souvenirs from Italy, then France, and then at last Germany, as the European campaign progressed. Packages sent from home often took circuitous routes, chasing after a soldier from battle front to battle front, island to island. Amidst all the chaos of the war, the arrival of such a package could seem like a miracle, and the lucky soldier to receive it might well cherish whatever heartfelt gift it carried for the rest of his life.*

*Sept 24, 1942*

*Virginia Racine Starns in 1942, shortly after she and Joe were married.*
*Joe Starns on September 24, 1942, the day he went overseas.*

# *Joseph and Virginia*
## STARNS

When Joe Starns reflects on the war years, he likes to quote a favorite line of poetry from John Milton: "They also serve who only stand and wait." To Joe, the role his wife, Virginia (who goes by Gina)—and so many other wives and mothers and sisters—played back home, and the love they sent to their men overseas, were at least as important to the war effort as the work of the soldiers themselves. The admiration Joe feels for Virginia and the strength with which she bore his absence, as well as the hard work and sacrifices she committed herself to during the war, are palpable in his voice when he talks about her. "She was saving every cent to buy war bonds, giving blood. They gave you a pin when you gave blood, and Gina has enough pins to fill a pincushion. She's only five feet two inches tall; she gave all the blood they'd let her give." As so many other couples did, Virginia and Joe met by a long-shot chance during the war, but their relationship quickly grew serious and has lasted for a very happy fifty-nine years.

One of five sons, Joe was raised in the San Joaquin Valley in California, near Modesto. During the course of the war, four of the five Starns boys would be shipped overseas, and luckily, all of them came back. As Joe says, "Unlike the five Sullivan brothers, all of whom were assigned to the same ship and all of whom perished when that ship was sunk, none of us ever had more than the vaguest notion where any of the others were or what mischief they were up to. But again, unlike the Sullivans, we all survived."

In early 1941, Joe was serving as an army private at the Presidio in
Monterey, California. In May he was temporarily assigned as a military
policeman in San Francisco, stationed at the Ferry Building. His main
duty was to greet incoming military personnel headed to the Presidio to
line up their transportation; he often helped them find overnight
accommodations and a meal. During the war, soldiers were sent on a
moment's notice from one base to another, to cities and towns they had
no knowledge of, and the military was trying to ease their confusion
upon arrival.

One day in May, nineteen-year-old Gina Racine and her older sister,
Mae, arrived in San Francisco by Greyhound bus from Manistee, Michigan, to stay with their older brother, who had moved there. They planned
to stay for some time and perhaps to even find jobs there. Their brother
lived in an apartment on Haight Street, which was much different in
those days from the notorious hippie haven it would become in the 1960s.
During their stay, Gina's brother often took her and Mae to the popular
Avalon Ballroom. One night there, Mae met a soldier named Ray Paul-
son, who was a buddy of Joe's. When Ray asked Mae for a second date,
she told him she'd go out with him again only if he brought a date for
her sister.

When Ray later told Joe that he had met two sisters from Michigan
who were visiting in San Francisco, and that he wanted Joe to escort the
younger sister on a double date, Joe was dubious. As he forthrightly says,
"Ray was a nice guy, but from what I knew of him, I figured the girls were
probably dogs." Ray persisted, however, and Joe eventually allowed himself to be corralled.

To his surprise, the girls were quite attractive, and they all had a very
good time. Gina was lively, petite, and very pretty, and Joe soon found
himself spending as much time as possible with her, often at the Avalon.
The last dance each night at the ballroom was danced to a song titled
"Avalon," which became "their song."

In September, Joe was transferred back to Monterey and from then
on was able to see Gina only when he could finagle a weekend pass. He
decided to make the most of one of those precious weekends, and on
October 31—Halloween and a night Gina remembers in jest as "fright

night"—he proposed to her. Gina readily accepted, but they held off on a date because Joe was still a private, earning only $50 a month, and wanted to be able to support her in better style.

In November, Joe was promoted to corporal and received a nice raise. In addition, Gina took a job in the money-order department of Western Union's main office in downtown San Francisco. Their income was now sufficient that they felt comfortable going ahead and getting married, but Joe's new job required him to be away from San Francisco quite a bit. He was assigned to escort trainloads of recruits from Monterey to various training camps in the Midwest and South. Many tentative wedding dates had to be forsaken when he found out he'd be on another trip.

Then, on the first Sunday in December, the "date which will live in infamy," Joe managed to get away from Monterey and went to visit Gina at her brother's house. He arrived early in the morning to be shocked by the news about the bombing of Pearl Harbor. They spent the rest of the day listening to radio reports about the attack, and they decided that they "had not heard" the repeated announcements that all military personnel should return immediately to their bases. Joe dreaded what he knew would follow, and he wanted to spend as much time with Gina as he could before facing the inevitable. He returned to base the next day, as originally scheduled, and nobody asked any questions.

Several months later, in March 1942, Gina recalls that "My willingness and the army's understanding all met on common ground. Joe was promoted to sergeant on the eighteenth, and he and I were married on the twenty-first, in one of those quickie little marriages that never last."

As a sergeant, Joe was making the grand sum of $78 a month, $54 of which went for rent on the small apartment he and Gina found for themselves. After only three weeks of marriage, however, Joe was shipped off for three months of infantry officer candidate school at Fort Benning, Georgia. He had volunteered for the infantry school because he felt he should play a more important role in the war effort. Upon graduation, he joined the infantry as what he calls "a second lieutenant of idiocy" on July 23, 1942—as he says, "only an idiot would join the infantry," with the highest mortality rate during the war. The insignia of the infantry was crossed rifles, which people called "idiot sticks."

Meanwhile, back in San Francisco, Gina had undergone "her own basic training"—learning to live alone without Joe. They wrote to each other often, but Gina hated being apart. After Joe graduated, he had to wait an undefined time in Georgia to find out where he would be sent. They had talked about her possibly coming to Georgia, but then one day Gina just decided she wasn't going to be away from him any longer. She called her office to say she was leaving and set off across the country by Greyhound bus. Though she sent several telegrams from the road, none of them arrived before she did. Joe's first inkling of her trip was when a soldier came into his barracks at Fort Benning—which Joe refers to as "Benning School for Boys"—and announced, to Joe's delight, "Lieutenant Starns, your wife is waiting for you."

When Joe's orders were finally issued—he would be going to the Pacific—the army sent him and Gina back to San Francisco pending his shipment out. They enjoyed that summer together, and then on September 24, 1942, Joe departed for the Pacific. Gina returned to her job at Western Union to endure the wait until he returned. She wrote to Joe every day for that duration, which turned out to be over three years. Joe says, "In all that time, she didn't write one demoralizing word, no matter what problems she was going through at home."

Gina not only sent heartening words, she sent thoughtful packages, too. Joe was an avid pipe smoker, and she regularly went to the tobacco store he loved, Sutliffs Tobacco Shop on Market Street, to buy his favorite tobacco, as well as occasionally a new pipe. She also sent him weekly bundles of the articles by his favorite columnist, Herb Caen of the *San Francisco Chronicle*. One especially fine gift she sent was a Longines wristwatch, as congratulations for his graduation from officer candidate school. Joe has always regretted that he lost this watch during the chaos of an air raid while he was serving in the Solomon Islands. But one of Gina's packages in particular stands out in Joe's mind; he still finds it remarkable that she could find the extra money for these items, with all the war bonds she was buying and their moderate income. Most stunning of all was the present she sent him in honor of their second wedding anniversary in 1944: a fourteen-karat gold ring with a black onyx stone and one small diamond. He actually received the ring on the day of their anniversary, and even more remarkable to Joe is that it fit his finger perfectly. He was in the midst of training in New Caledonia before heading to the Philippines, which everyone knew would be a brutal battle. To receive that ring at such a time, and to have it slide onto his finger and miraculously fit just right, was a deeply emotional moment he has cherished all of his life. He has never taken the ring off since that day.

Gina's packages arrived erratically, often several at once: They had to follow Joe all over the Pacific, to Hawaii, Guadalcanal, New Georgia; back to Guadalcanal, on to New Zealand, up to New Caledonia, then to the Philippines. Joe's experience in the Pacific, like that of so many thousands of American soldiers, sailors, and marines, included a litany of famous island battles, but also like many veterans, he prefers not to discuss those experiences. What he does like to reflect on are two remarkable coincidences that have always stood out in his mind.

In 1942, Joe's seventeen-year-old younger brother was serving in the navy on the U.S.S. *Northampton,* which was taking part in the battle for Guadalcanal. One night the ship was torpedoed and sank. Joe's brother made it off the ship, then floated in the dark for nine hours in his life jacket before he was finally rescued and transported to a naval hospital in Noumea, New Caledonia, where he recuperated for three weeks before being sent back to the States. During the time Joe's brother lay in his hospital bed, looking out at the anchored ships, the troopship transporting Joe to Guadalcanal stopped over at Noumea. The troops were allowed off the ship one day, and Joe remembers aimlessly wandering around, having no idea that his little brother lay right there in the hospital.

Three years later, in early June 1945, Joe's even younger brother, then just sixteen years old, was serving in the merchant marine. His cargo ship docked in the harbor at Tacloban, on Leyte in the Philippines, where it laid over for about three weeks. The crew were free to leave the ship, and Joe's brother had received word that Joe's infantry unit was at that time in combat about 125 miles north of Manila on Luzon island.

Determined to try to find Joe, but with no means of transportation to Luzon, on June 8, he hitchhiked and actually managed to reach Joe's company's command post, arriving on June 8. But, to his great disappointment, he got there only to learn that just a few hours before, Joe suffered a serious leg wound and was evacuated to a hospital. Joe's brother sadly turned back toward his ship at Tacloban, but he did not return the way he had come. Instead, he worked his way to an airfield, Nichols Field, in Manila, where he finagled a ride on an Air Force transport to the airstrip at Tacloban, near the harbor where his ship was docked. Remarkably, Joe was making the very same journey: He was processed through a series of medical facilities until he arrived at, where else, Nichols Field, and was flown from there to none other than the field hospital at the Tacloban airstrip. For the next two weeks, while Joe lay in his hospital bed looking out at the ships in the harbor, his brother was on one of those ships not a half mile away. Joe and his brothers knew nothing of any of these coincidences until they were reunited in 1945 after the war and started sharing their war stories.

The coincidences don't stop there, however. Joe's leg wound was serious enough that the war was over for him, and a long period of recuperation lay ahead. He was sent back to the States, and on July 5 he arrived at the hospital at Hamilton Air Force Base just north of San Francisco. Gina had received no word as yet of Joe's injury, but that very morning before she left for work, she received a dreaded telegram from the War Department. Just as she was signing for the telegram, with the anxiety growing that it would carry horrible news, her telephone rang. In one hand she held the unopened telegram, and with the other she answered the phone—to find to her great joy that it was Joe calling from Hamilton Air Force Base. The first thing she did after she got off the phone was call her office at Western Union and quit her job. Then she tried desperately to find a cab to take her up to Hamilton, and when she couldn't, she rented a limousine for the then-princely sum of $35. As Joe says fondly, "It seemed to me like a pretty big car for such a little lady."

Joe Starns received a Silver Star for his service in the Pacific. Gina actually read about it in the *San Francisco Chronicle* before he'd been told. Joe remained in the army after his recuperation; he fought in Korea and was stationed for some time in Japan, where Gina and their four children joined him. He and Gina are proud to say that they now have five grand-children.

With great admiration, Joe points out that the house they have now lived in for 42 years was bought with the use of all those war bonds Gina saved up for while he was overseas.

*Joe as an army private in 1941, while courting Gina. He was on duty at the Ferry Building at the foot of Market Street in San Francisco.*

*Gina and Sergeant Joe on their wedding day, March 21, 1942.*

*The telegram that made up Gina's mind not to wait for the army to make up its mind, and to join Joe in Georgia.*

WESTERN UNION

1201

CLASS OF SERVICE

This is a full-rate Telegram or Cablegram unless its deferred character is indicated by a suitable symbol above or preceding the address.

SYMBOLS

DL = Day Letter
NT = Overnight Telegram
"Deferred Cable
=Cable Night Letter
Ship Radiogram

A. N. WILLIAMS
PRESIDENT

NEWCOMB CARLTON
CHAIRMAN OF THE BOARD

J. C. WILLEVER
FIRST VICE-PRESIDENT

The filing time shown in the date line on telegrams and day letters is STANDARD TIME at point of origin. Time of receipt is STANDARD TIME at point of destination

FJ8 35  NT= COLUMBUS GA 25

MRS JOE E STARNS=

APT 3 1344 GEARY ST=

DARLING, GOT MY ORDERS TODAY, BUT DONT KNOW JUST WHEN
I LEAVE. COMING TO COAST SOON THOUGH. LOVE YOU AN AWFUL
LOT HONEY AND WILL BE SEEING YOU SOON. SO LONG FOR A
WHILE DARLING=

JOE.

THE COMPANY WILL APPRECIATE SUGGESTIONS FROM ITS PATRONS CONCERNING ITS SERVICE

Joe, now a lieu-
tenant, in 1944 in
New Caledonia
during training
for the invasion
of Luzon. A
photograph of
Gina sits on
his desk.

Lieutenant Colonel Joe
with Gina, at right, at
his retirement ceremony in
1958, seventeen years, two
wars, and four children
after they met.

Gina, Joe, and their oldest
daughter, Sharon, on Christmas
Day 2000. Gina was seventy-
eight and Joe eighty-two at
the time.

THOUGH SO MANY GREAT ROMANCES
took off immediately during the war, others
took longer to develop and were sometimes
based almost entirely on letters. A young man might
find himself seriously smitten by a woman who wasn't
sure she wanted to commit to him or any one man
right away. To make sure her correspondent understood this, the woman might make casual mention in
her letters of various other boyfriends. That didn't
necessarily mean that the man on the receiving end
could stop hoping that one day there would be more
between the two of them.

*Ned and Nikki Burr with Nikki's mother,*
*Lyra Nicholas, the day of their wedding,*
*December 21, 1947.*

# *Edward and Patricia*
## BURR

---

At Christmastime in 1942, Ned Burr, a senior at West Point due to graduate in June, came home to Garden City, Long Island, to spend the holidays with his family. While there, he bumped into an old friend from grammar school days, Dud Whitney, who suggested they go into Manhattan on a double date. Dud Whitney's date was a girl named Nikki Nicholas (Patricia was called by this nickname) from Douglaston, Long Island. After Ned's graduation, Dud and Ned double-dated again, and again Dud brought Nikki Nicholas.

Before Ned left for training at Fort Sill, Oklahoma, his mother gave a small party to which Dud and Nikki were invited. Ned's mother was quite taken with Nikki, and in the tradition of "Mother knows best"—even though Nikki was there with another man—she told the young woman she should marry her son. Her reasoning? "Nikki and Ned" would look great written together on Christmas cards, she said, only half jokingly. Ned's mother encouraged Nikki to write to Ned while he was attending artillery school in Oklahoma, where he would be for the next three months. Nineteen-year-old Nikki did just that, later maintaining that at the time she was interested merely in adding a West Pointer to her rather long list of boyfriends.

That first letter was the start of a voluminous correspondence—over 140 letters in all—that lasted until March 1946 and which Ned refers to as his "wooing from a distance." Nikki and Ned saw each other face-to-face for only two more brief interludes before he was sent overseas. In October 1943, Ned briefly returned home to Long Island en route to joining the Eighty-third Division in Kentucky for training. He visited again in February of the following year. "We probably had no more than eight dates during those two visits," Ned recalls. But the letters that passed between them created a strong bond. Though Nikki's letters to Ned were lost—it was difficult for soldiers at the front to hang on to anything except their fighting equipment—when reading a sample of the letters Ned wrote to her, one doesn't question why she kept writing him back.

Just before Ned was shipped overseas on April 3, 1944, he wrote a beautiful letter to Nikki, an excerpt of which reads:

> Nikki, when the going gets tough and the morale gets a little low, my thoughts are coming back to you like a homing pigeon. I'll try to write every day, even though they may not reach you each day. I can easily admit that not seeing you again has been a hard blow to swallow. (I try to figure ahead of time on what to write, but there doesn't seem to be much question as you are the letter). Do I bore you with this continuous topic? Don't answer that for it won't do you any good. . . . Again and again I can profess my love for you, but never will I be able to describe the loveliness and the pain I find in the moments when my thoughts are with you—never will I be able to make you know how much I will miss you while I'm gone.

The Eighty-third Division in which Ned was serving was one of the most battle-tested in Europe. Three days after the division relieved the 101st Airborne Division just south of Carentan in Normandy, Ned was ordered up to the front as a forward observer with the 331st Infantry Regiment. From there, on June 30, he wrote a letter that conveys vividly how much the letters he received from Nikki meant to him, as well as how much he was hoping that she would decide, before long, that he was the one for her:

> My Dearest Nikki:
>     I fell upon your letter today like a ton of bricks. The blue envelope has become well known and its arrival is heralded far and wide.

The biggest events in my life right now are the comings of your thoughts. With all this other stuff going on, I can truthfully say your letters mean more than all of it. Not just the fact of receiving word from you, but the idea of being closer to you . . . I search each and every letter for slightest indication that you have decided. Before, we may have had too little time to decide if what we felt was love, but I've thought of you far too often and yearned to be with you far too much for it to be anything else as far as I'm concerned.

However, I can afford to commit myself, while it's definitely not the best idea for you. It's a dangerous game we play and one's number can be up almost any time. Such unpleasant closeness to death and scenes of it around you don't increase your bravery or eating abilities. I'm satisfied though, now, that I can do my job in the face of it and that's the main thing. No matter what anyone thinks, you must be satisfied yourself of your nerve before you can feel content. You'd be surprised how much you help.

On the fourth of July, the Eighty-third Division began its attack on the entrenched Germans in the hedgerow country of Normandy. They were untested soldiers going up against veteran German troops, and the consequences were horrendous: the Eighty-third lost seventeen hundred men on the first day of the assault alone, and many more in the days that followed. Ned was seriously wounded that first day when a shell landed close to him and a fragment of it ripped into his back below his left shoulder, exiting just above his heart. He was transported to a hospital in England. When he recovered, he rejoined his division and stayed with it until it was deactivated in Austria in February 1946.

NIKKI WAS the only girl Ned wrote to during the war, but he knew that she dated a number of men during the two years he was fighting in Europe, and had even developed two serious relationships. The second of these was in full bloom when Ned was deactivated. "My last letter to Nikki in March of 1946, sent from Gmunden, Austria, sort of closed out our relationship, since I felt that too much of her life didn't involve me anymore. How wrong I was!"

When Ned returned to America in March 1946, he was sent to a pro-

*Ned's West Point graduation photo.*

*Ned (kneeling third from left) with, left to right, Lieutenants Beard, Bradford, and Leonard in Normandy in late June 1944.*

*Christmas card with the "Nikki & Ned" signature Ned's mother thought would look so good, sent from Albuquerque in 1947.*

*Nikki and Ned in 1998.*

cessing center at Fort Dix, New Jersey. Immediately upon his arrival there he gave Nikki a call at *The New York Times,* where she worked, just to say hello. She agreed to meet him at Grand Central Station. "We got into a cab, started kissing, and forty-five days later, when I had to return to Europe, we were engaged. We were married on December twenty-first, 1946, and will celebrate our fifty-fifth year together this December."

ILLIONS OF AMERICAN servicemen carried pictures of their sweethearts and wives with them during the war. Some carried pictures of girls they barely knew, girls they'd maybe danced with a few times; anything to provide a distraction from the war. Girls were happy to supply these pictures, each of which soon found itself tucked in a soldier's pocket, some at the front in a foreign land. Pictures of movie stars adorned barracks and offices everywhere, even bulkheads above the bunks of ships at sea. Betty Grable and Rita Hayworth were the favorite pinups. Occasionally the boys would pin up a picture of a girl who was not a movie star nor even anyone's sweetheart: just a pretty girl whose smile suggested that home was a place you could return to, some happy day.

*Paul and Frieda Kincade at dinner following their
wedding on December 23, 1945.*

# *Paul and Frieda*

## KINCADE

In February 1942, Paul Kincade was at navy boot camp in San Diego, California, sleeping in the top bunk adjacent to the table where other recruits sat to write letters home. Paul had grown up in San Diego and had no need to write letters to distant relatives, but he often sat on his bunk at night and kibitzed with those who did write. One night, a sailor writing home had his wallet open on the tabletop. Paul couldn't help noticing a picture of a gorgeous young woman. "I asked him if it was his wife," Paul remembers, "and he said, no, it wasn't. I asked if it was his girl-friend, and he said it was his cousin Frieda. Tongue in cheek, I told him, sure, every sailor carries his cousin's picture in his wallet. When he swore it was his cousin, I called his bluff and asked for her address." To Paul's surprise, the sailor wrote out the address and gave it to him.

"I put the address in my writing portfolio and proceeded to forget about it. After boot camp, I was assigned to signalman-quartermaster school for twelve weeks and was kept too busy to write letters. When we completed our training in early June, the entire class was issued orders to the naval armed guard—Atlantic, out of Brooklyn, to sail on armed mer-chant ships in convoy. We were ordered to empty our lockers and pack our seabags and hammocks to await the arrival of trucks to take us to the train station. As I opened the locker door, my writing portfolio tumbled out, and out of it fell that slip of paper with Frieda's address. Having some time to kill, I sat down and wrote her a letter, telling her about myself and asking if she would be interested in corresponding with me."

Paul and his fellow sailors took a cross-country train ride to New York, which became his home port. In July 1942 he was assigned to a newly commissioned Liberty Ship, the *Thomas Sumter*, out of Philadelphia. From there, he was assigned to a number of different ships and was never in one place long enough to have a mailing address, so when he finally returned to New York after several months, he picked up a huge pile of back mail. Among the letters he found a reply from Frieda, who had enclosed a photograph of herself. "She wrote such a warm letter that I rushed to respond, starting a long-distance correspondence that would go on for two and a half years before we ever met."

Paul was an artist and cartoonist, and he drew a pencil sketch of Frieda from the first photo she sent. He still has the photo, but he had to give up the sketch. When he was assigned to a British merchant ship, Paul taped the sketch to the bulkhead above his bunk so that he could lie there and gaze up at it. His two merchant marine roommates liked the sketch, too. "When I detached from the ship in Trinidad, the cadets wouldn't let me take the drawing," Paul remembers. "They, too, had fallen for Frieda's beauty. So I left it with them. Just three days later, the British ship MV *King James* left Trinidad and was torpedoed and sunk between Trinidad and Tobago, losing all hands except for the third mate and one of the British gun crew, and taking Frieda's picture to the bottom, where I presume it still rests."

In December 1944, Paul arrived in San Francisco, where he would wait for a new assignment that was highly classified. San Francisco was Frieda's hometown, and Paul took advantage of the opportunity to finally meet her face-to-face. Their first date was on the third anniversary of Pearl Harbor, December 7. They went to a movie, along with another sailor whom Frieda had asked Paul to bring along as a blind date for her girlfriend—he assumed she didn't want to be alone with him on their first meeting, despite all the letters they had exchanged. They went to see the John Wayne picture *They Were Expendable*. "It was," Paul says, "love at first sight, strengthened by two and a half years of an increasingly loving correspondence." In fact, as their letter writing progressed, Frieda had taken to marking her letters with her lipstick imprint, a gesture "popular among young women in those war years," according to Paul.

After just a couple of weeks, Paul had no doubts that Frieda was the woman for him; she felt the same way, and they became engaged. On Christmas Eve, they announced their engagement to friends and relatives. Just days later, Paul got word that he and the other troops waiting in San Francisco were being sent to Tanforan Racetrack in San Bruno, California, to train for their new assignment, which they still knew almost nothing about. In the interim they were sent to Treasure Island, off the coast of San Francisco, to a high-security compound with barbed wire and armed guards. They could neither make nor receive phone calls, receive or send mail. Paul was distressed because he had a movie date with Frieda that night, and he feared that when she showed up and he was gone, without word, she would think he had skipped out on her. Fortunately, a neighbor of Frieda's, whom Paul had met, was serving as a guard at Treasure Island. Paul managed to call him over and ask him to get word to Frieda that he still loved her and would contact her at the first opportunity.

Not for weeks, after he had been flown to Barber's Point Naval Air Station at Manus, in the Admiralty Islands, did Paul find out what his new assignment was. At a meeting in Quebec in late 1944, Winston Churchill had offered units of the Royal Navy to Roosevelt to aid in the decimating Pacific campaign. Paul and the others were being assigned to British ships, which were far below United States Navy standards. They were told the navy would be supplying special rations for them, as well as athletic equipment and American cigarettes, and also that each day they served would count double for rotation back to the States. None of these promises ever materialized. They were trained by war-wounded marines for first-wave landing, to set up panel markers on the beach, very dangerous work. But Paul managed to come back alive.

"I got back to San Francisco almost a year to the day after we first met, and we set our wedding date for December twenty-third, 1945. Because I wouldn't convert to her religion [Russian Orthodox—Frieda was of Albanian heritage], we couldn't get married in her church, and I became the bad guy with her family for not converting. Instead, we had a lovely wedding in a nearby Lutheran church, marred only by her mother's refusal to attend [her father had passed away in 1943]."

When they got engaged the year before, Paul had promised Frieda that they would spend their wedding night in one of the finest hotels in

San Francisco. But just before the wedding, the woman at the Military Hotel Reservation Bureau told Paul that even though the war was over, a hotel room in the city was impossible to get without booking two months in advance. "I told her about the promise I'd made and related my sad tale about being assigned to a ship of the Royal Navy, which came from the cold climes of the North Atlantic without being refitted for the heat and humidity of the central Pacific; how there'd been no food and I'd lost thirty pounds; and added in the daily kamikaze attacks. She said, 'You poor dear,' and picked up the phone to call the Mark Hopkins. I could hear the laughter at the other end, but the lady told my story of woe, and when she hung up, she said, 'Honey, grab a cab and get over to the hotel and make a deposit. She's holding a room for you.' I ran out, bought that nice lady a box of chocolates, and then raced to the Mark, as everyone called it. I was told the room rate was fifteen dollars and paid it in full." Paul notes that a double room these days is listed "in the AAA tour book at $380 to $475 a night!"

After the wedding, Paul's new brother-in-law drove the couple straight to the Mark, dropping them off after midnight. "When we walked into the lobby, we saw a huge Christmas tree surrounded by a host of drunks singing carols. A number of others were passed out around the lobby. There was no one at the registration desk, so I kept hitting the little bell for service. A man came to the desk and asked what I wanted. I told him I was registered, so he looked in the book and told me I didn't have a reservation. I showed him my receipt and told him we had just gotten married and weren't going to spend the night sleeping in the park. He said not to get excited; he wasn't the desk clerk but the house detective. There'd been a hotel party to celebrate the first postwar Christmas, and the clerk was passed out in his office. The house detective told me the only room available was a suite costing fifty dollars. When I balked at the price, he told me I had already paid, so we enjoyed a lovely suite overlooking the city by the bay."

Paul soon returned to his military duties. He got out of the navy in 1947 but stayed in the reserves and rejoined in 1952. He was commissioned as an officer in 1957 and retired in 1968 as a lieutenant commander. Despite the separations inevitable in a navy career—and the presentiment on the part of Frieda's family that the marriage wouldn't last—Paul is proud to say, "Our marriage persevered, and Frieda did an outstanding job of raising our two sons."

In 1990, on their forty-fifth wedding anniversary, Paul wrote to the general manager of the Mark Hopkins and told him the story of their wedding night there. Jokingly, Paul asked what the chances were of getting a $15 room so many years later. "To my utter surprise, he replied, 'What an interesting story. To think you were married forty-five years ago and spent your honeymoon in the Mark and are still married. It would be our pleasure to honor the fifteen-dollar-per-night rate for as long as you wish to stay with us. And, of course, you will be our guests in the dining room.' I hadn't told my wife I was writing that letter, and when I showed her the reply, she said, 'You didn't ask them to give you a room at the Mark for fifteen dollars a night, did you?' Unfortunately, we were unable to go at that time and had to skip the offer."

After his retirement from the service, Paul took classes in psychology and became a diplomate in psychology. He worked as a forensic hypnotist with the San Diego Police Department for twenty-two years, and currently he is a reserve detective with the Washoe County Sheriff's Office in Reno, Nevada. He was inducted into the International Hypnosis Hall of Fame for work with law-enforcement agencies all over the United States and also with Mexico.

He and Frieda had been married over forty-eight years when she died in 1994. Reflecting on the happy life they shared, Paul comments that "ours was indeed a love story that ended only when 'death did us part.'"

*Paul Kincade in 1942 while waiting in Mobile, Alabama, to be assigned to a new merchant ship.*

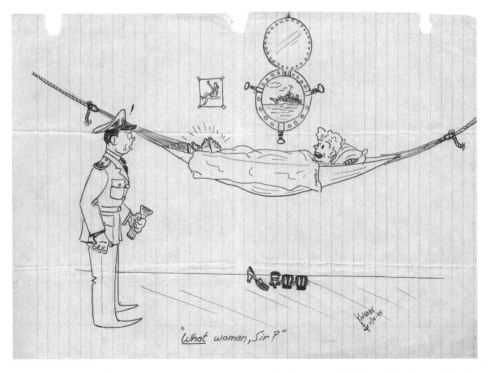

*One of many cartoons Paul enclosed with his letters to Frieda while he was in the NJROTC unit at Yale University in 1944 before, as he writes, "they realized their mistake and sent me back to the sea and the British Pacific Fleet!"*

*A painting Paul had made while he was stationed in Japan in 1959, from the photograph of Frieda that her cousin gave him.*

*Paul carrying the U.S. flag at the head of the "Pass By," or parade, in Portsmouth, England, at the fiftieth reunion of the British Pacific Fleet. Paul was the only "Yank," as he says, out of the over fifteen thousand veterans, and he wore his Stetson and boots so that everyone would know he was American.*

M ILITARY BASES WERE LOCATED *all over the country, especially along the coastlines, but the greatest concentration of training camps was in the South, where the warmer weather made year-round training more manageable. Hundreds of thousands of young men who had seldom traveled outside their own states suddenly found themselves in an entirely different part of the country. Many couples met at USO dances organized in the towns and cities near these bases. Often the girl who stood out from the crowd was a local resident, but sometimes she, too, was from another part of the country, uprooted by the war.*

*Bea and John Sutherland while he was stationed
at Turner Field in Albany, Georgia, in 1944.*

# J. W. and Bea
## SUTHERLAND

John Wesley Sutherland was a private in the army air force in 1942, stationed at Seymour Johnson Field in Goldsboro, North Carolina. He went by the name of Johnny back then. Like most GIs, he couldn't wait for the USO dances held in town every weekend. On one of those Saturday nights, he became transfixed by a junior hostess he'd never seen before. "My eyes nearly popped out of my head," Johnny recalls. "She was the prettiest girl on earth. I even remember what she had on that night: a white blouse, a black skirt, and a wide red belt. There were always more soldiers than girls at the dances, so I had to keep cutting in. She thought that was funny. I was kind of a shy boy, but I just couldn't help myself."

The name of the stunning girl was Beatrice Victoria Kalayjian. She was originally from South Dakota but was working in Goldsboro as an X-ray technician for two local doctors. After cutting in several times, Johnny finally summoned the courage to ask Bea for a date—for the very next day. She taught Sunday school and invited him to join her for church services, which he did with pleasure. They had lunch after church and spent the rest of the afternoon together.

During November and December of that year, Johnny and Bea went on about six dates, culminating in a Christmas Day dinner at the house where Bea lived; her landlady, Mrs. Harrell, had invited Johnny to join them. After dinner, when Bea went into the kitchen to help with the preparations, wise Mrs. Harrell told her to get right back out to the living room. She was sure Johnny was going to propose to Bea. "How she knew that, I'll never know," Johnny says, chuckling. But that was indeed his intention, since he had orders to report to Boca Raton, Florida, for officer's training school on January 1, 1943, only a week away. "Bea wanted time to think it over," he recalls, "as well she should have. She was as smart then as she is now."

During his nine weeks of training in Florida, John wrote to Bea every day, plus a special delivery on Sunday, and she finally agreed to marry him. "The best letter I ever received," he says. When Bea told her father she was engaged, and that her fiancé's name was John Wesley Sutherland, her father replied that he must be a fine fellow, to have such a good Methodist name. (John Wesley, of course, founded Methodism with his brother Charles at Oxford, England, in 1729.) It still amuses John that in fact, he was named after his father, who was Baptist.

In March, shortly after they became engaged, John was transferred to New Haven, Connecticut, where the army air force had taken over part of Yale University. He was being trained as a maintenance officer. Bea and John set their wedding date for July 3, 1943, with the ceremony to be held in the Yale Chapel. Until the wedding, Bea stayed with her sister Marian in New York City, because she could travel easily from there to see John in New Haven.

Given the often helter-skelter circumstances of weddings in those strenuous days, when many ceremonies were quickie registry-office affairs, Bea and John felt lucky to be getting married by an air force chaplain in the beautiful Yale Chapel. "You couldn't ask for a lovelier place to get married," Bea remembers wistfully. In those days, families were often unable to travel to the ceremony, but Bea's father, a doctor in South Dakota, managed to get there, as did one of her brothers, her sister Marian, and other friends and family. None of John's family, however, could attend. John did at least have a good friend there, a fellow cadet from Arkansas named Fred Venable, to serve as his best man.

Though John and Bea had only a one-night honeymoon, their surroundings weren't too shabby for that, either: the Waldorf-Astoria in New York, then as now one of the most famous hotels in the world. "When John told me where we were going for our honeymoon, I almost fainted," Bea says with a laugh.

About two weeks after the wedding, John graduated as a second lieutenant, and he and Bea left by train for Maxwell Field in Montgomery, Alabama. He was then posted to Turner Field in Albany, Georgia, where they spent almost two years. Their daughter, Sue Fann, was born in Alice, Texas, after the war. "The light of our lives," John proclaims.

John and Bea Sutherland celebrated their fifty-seventh anniversary in July 2000. Their rich life together includes four grandchildren and three great-grandchildren. They've traveled abroad and visited all fifty states over the years, and have a network of friends and family across the continent. They are both great music fans and attend performances all over the country. They are particularly fond of opera and have enjoyed productions at all the major American opera houses and festivals, from New York's Metropolitan Opera to the San Francisco Opera House. When John retired from business nearly twenty years ago, they were free to travel at all times of the year. They're the kind of people who will make a trip several hundred miles out of their way to catch a Pennsylvania performance by the son of a second cousin starring in a production of Neil Simon's *The Odd Couple.*

The chance encounter in North Carolina of a young private from Texas and an X-ray technician from South Dakota never would have occurred if it hadn't been for World War II. "This may sound corny," declares John, "but to have found Bea at a USO dance—of all places— was the best thing that ever happened to me.

"I've read that the secret of a good marriage is one double bed and two bathrooms," John notes with amusement, but his and Bea's shared fondness for bridge games, travel, and fine music have had a lot to do with it as well.

All things considered, it was good that Bea was wearing that very noticeable wide red belt one Saturday night nearly sixty years ago in Goldsboro, North Carolina.

*Private John Sutherland in 1942 at Seymour Johnson Field in Goldsboro, North Carolina.*

*Bea and John cutting their wedding cake at their reception in New York City on July 3, 1943.*

*Bea and John on their fiftieth wedding anniversary, July 3, 1993.*

THE LOVE AFFAIRS KINDLED AT SO many USO dances came to many different ends. Some of these whirlwind romances intensified during the war through deeply felt letters, and many culminated in marriage. But even if marriage wasn't the ultimate outcome, sometimes those relationships, and those wonderful letters, were cherished for years and years.

*Anne Hetrick in her senior prom gown, with Lieutenant Harry Greissman in his uniform from the Seventy- eighth ("Lightning") Division in May 1943.*

# Anne Hetrick
## KENNEDY

Though Anne Hetrick was only eighteen in the summer of 1942, she was about to begin her senior year at Winthrop College in Rock Hill, South Carolina, not far from her hometown of Walhalla. As was fairly common in her generation, Anne had skipped a grade in elementary school, and at that time in South Carolina, there were only eleven grades. So Anne had entered college when she was just fifteen. She was spending this summer away from home in Raleigh, North Carolina, with her mother, who was there taking care of Anne's uncle, her mother's brother, who was ill. Though Anne's parents were still married, her father had moved back to his native Pennsylvania several years earlier because the hosiery mills his family owned in various towns in the South had failed during the Depression. Anne's mother, Ida, "couldn't abide" the North, and she stayed behind in Walhalla with Anne when he moved.

Anne was a poised and very pretty young lady with soft brown hair. While in Raleigh, she answered the call of the USO, whose slogan was "Morale is *your* job," and regularly attended the dances held that summer at the Memorial Auditorium. On one August evening, Anne met two different soldiers named Harry, who were friends. At first Anne was more attracted to Harry Claeyssens, because, as she recalls, he was such a "dashing dancer." But she dated both, and as time went on, Anne gradually realized that the other Harry appealed to her more. He might not have been as great a dancer as Harry Claeyssens, but Harry Greissman, who hailed from Brooklyn, could "make words sing." Whether talking or putting words on paper, he had a poet's instinct for the evocative phrase and the telling detail that illuminated a place or a feeling.

First Lieutenant Harry Greissman was twenty-four and a graduate of City College of New York. He spoke fluent German—his parents were immigrants—and he taught the language to other young officers at Camp Butner, North Carolina, where he was stationed during 1942 and '43. He was a member of the Seventy-eighth Division, famous as the "Lightning Division" during World War I and reconstituted as a World War II training unit.

Camp Butner was only thirty miles from Raleigh, and when Anne returned to college in South Carolina, Harry wrote letters and visited her at Rock Hill when he had weekend leave. She also saw him back in Raleigh when she visited her mother, who had decided to stay after the summer. Anne would almost always go to a dance there, with her mother as chaperone. Because her mother enjoyed entertaining—she had been a home economics major in college, graduating in 1918—she started to invite the soldiers Anne met at the dances and some of their friends back to her house to stay overnight and have a home-cooked Sunday dinner. Her mother's house had six bedrooms, and the soldiers loved the opportunity to spend time in a comfortable home, as well as the luxury of staying in Raleigh instead of crowding into the cramped buses that returned to the bases. Harry stayed over at Anne's mother's house several times when Anne was visiting, and he sometimes accompanied Anne back to college on the train.

In Rock Hill, Harry and Anne would sometimes spend time with Anne's aunt Kate, who was a music teacher at the college and lived a few blocks from the campus. Her aunt once asked Anne if, when she and Harry sat on the porch swing at her house, she allowed any "liberties." Anne explains with amusement that in those astonishingly innocent times, what her aunt meant by liberties was holding hands, which she and Harry most certainly did not do. But as time went on, Harry did begin calling Anne "darling" in the many letters he wrote to her, letters that Anne cherishes to this day.

His letters during this period say little about his army experience and instead talk about life apart from the war. Harry aspired to become a journalist, a dream that generated considerable enthusiasm for a James Cagney movie he managed to catch one weekend, *Johnny Come Lately.* "You and I shall see this picture together many times over, darlin'," he wrote to Anne. "It is the simple picture of every newspaperman's credo—with nary an ounce of sentimentality, it drives home the place of an honest newspaper in a small town, its place as a pleader of causes, some lost some won, but all bravely fought. The picture is racy as h—— and had moments of hilarity that nearly tore my ribs out—I don't remember laughing so long and loudly since the time I put the ketchup into my coffee instead of [on] the ham sandwich."

Though Anne loved Harry's writing, and she had come to love him, he was not the only soldier she corresponded with during the war. She was an avid letter writer and kept up extensive correspondences with several young men. Anne absolutely loved to dance, and with so many dances going on during the war, she danced with more soldiers than she could count. Many a soldier must have fallen a little in love with her, a standout in her favorite ball gown, and many of them wrote to her after meeting her. If they wrote, she wrote back as long as the letters kept coming.

One air force lieutenant she corresponded with, Alfred M. Kelly, traveled all the way from Florida, where he had been stationed, to attend her college graduation. His next base assignment was to a Pacific island, the name of which had to be withheld in his letters. Letters kept arriving for a time after he had shipped to the Pacific, but then they stopped, and Anne has never known for sure whether he met some other girl or, as she feared, was killed.

Through 1942 and '43, Anne also maintained a correspondence with her old hometown boyfriend, Jim Hughes, who was cocaptain of the football team at Newberry College in South Carolina. He even came up to Rock Hill and later, to Raleigh, to visit her. He entered the service, becoming an ensign in the navy, and she lost touch with him after he went overseas. For years she had no word of him but has since learned that he survived the war, went on to marry and have two children, and moved back to South Carolina.

Once, knowing how much soldiers liked to receive gifts from home, Anne tried to knit a sweater for one of her correspondents, but she says, laughing, "It turned out to be a sleeping bag." So she settled for writing her "fingers to the shoulder blades" instead. Dear Dan, Dear Joe, Dear Bill, Dear Al, Dear Ashby, and on and on. As much as all of these young men meant to her, when it came to love, there was only Harry.

As the war dragged on, more soldiers were needed at the front lines, and the Seventy-eighth began the transition from a training to a fighting unit. In February 1944, Harry's division was sent to Nashville, Tennessee, for two months of exhausting war games in what seemed to Harry like endless rain, "infinitely worse than snow," he wrote, "a cold, clammy rain, turning the best of roads (and most of those are the worst) into slippery trails to treacherous cliffs."

But Harry had some wry stories to tell, too. "Notice the new point on my pen? Yesterday, I managed to steal time to take a haircut in a real civilian barber shop, and while he was clipping my hair, the barber recited the sad tale of a soldier trying to work his way home on a furlough, with a pen as his only asset. The kindly barber gave the GI $4 for his pen, and then recalled his own illiteracy. He tried to trade the pen in for a shovel and failing that, decided to sell it. So, in the process of being clipped about the scalp, I emerged with a new pen but the same old scrawl."

Then the Seventy-eighth made the trip up to Camp Pickett in Virginia, a four-day convoy trip filled with tension: Every soldier knew that from there, you were certain to be shipped overseas. Sure enough, most of the soldiers in the convoy were shipped out to Europe for D-Day preparations. Harry and some of the other officers remained at Fort Pickett through the spring and into the summer, but he knew he'd be going across the Atlantic before long.

In mid-October, Harry was on his way over, and he wrote a letter to Anne while aboard ship. He had been listening to someone play "As Time Goes By" on the piano. *Casablanca* had been thrown together in a hurry for its release in 1942, but it was already a classic, and its bittersweet song could be heard everywhere. Harry noted that the pianist wasn't very good, but the music cast its spell even so: "As time goes by," he wrote to Anne, "the tide carries all of us farther and farther from the things each of us loves best." Back home, Anne read his words with a little trepidation. She knew that Harry wanted her to commit to him, but she was only twenty and just wasn't ready yet.

Though Harry narrowly escaped the carnage of D-Day, he soon

found himself plunged into the Battle of the Bulge, the largest land battle
of the war. This German offensive, fought in the forested area of Belgium
and Luxembourg known as the Ardennes, caught the Allies by surprise—
the idea had astonished Hitler's generals when he first brought it up in
September 1944. The German military command knew they faced plenty
of challenge just trying to prevent invasion by the Allied forces, let alone
trying to launch an attack. They pleaded with Hitler to abandon the plan,
but he refused. At five-thirty A.M. on December 16, 1944, eight German
armored divisions and thirteen infantry divisions launched an all-out
attack on five divisions of the United States First Army. The Americans'
losses that first day were staggering, but they quickly regrouped to block
the German advance. Though the official military name of the battle was
the Battle of the Ardennes, the frontline Americans referred to it as the
Battle of the Bulge, because of the way the German line bulged out
toward them. Journalists began using that moniker in their reports, and
the name stuck forever.

Harry was a forward observer during the battle. His job was to call in
artillery where it was needed, and he was stationed very close to the front.
Amid all of the hellish carnage, he hunkered down on Christmas Day
and wrote a truly remarkable letter to Anne:

MY DARLING, I have just seen and heard something that I shall never
forget, and there is SO much to remember already: Christmas services in a winter woodland blanketed with snow and ice, shattered by
cannon and small arms fire. Above the cannon's roar and the angry
spitfire of machine guns and rifles, you can still hear the still, small
voice of an organ piping hymns forever old and new. It was a congre-
gation that continued to wear steel helmets and side arms, and hand
grenades still dangled brazenly from many a shoulder harness—but
the Lord surely saw no blasphemy here—a more devout company
never came to worship! Many a face was dirty and bearded and eyes
gleamed across the organ notes through slits narrowed by nights with
little sleep and less rest. And in the gallant company none was more
brave than this chaplain, whose name I do not even know, for they
tell me that he is wherever the fighting is. . . .

The last notes of the last hymn are dying into the distance now, darling, and each of that strange company is now returning to his separate duty, and yet as I too turn away from the heavens to hell again, I can not help but think that we are all of us alike, the chaplain and the rest of us, each serving God and country according to the manner set forth by the destiny beyond us all. . . .

Some of Harry's other communications from the front were of a different nature. He sent a set of Christmas cards, one depicting Hitler as a snowman with GIs throwing snowballs at him. Another card poked some fun at the U.S. Army command, with Sergeant George Baker's famous "Sad Sack" character carrying a huge bag filled with Santa's toys, while the general behind him strolled along unencumbered.

As American troops moved forward into Germany during the next few months, Anne received a number of packages from Harry. He sent wads of German money from the days of the Weimar Republic, just before Hitler rose to power. These bills were worth little enough during the days of the republic, due to tremendous inflation, and were utterly devoid of value now. GIs were constantly finding caches of the bills in the walls of bombed-out houses, where they had been hidden in the hope that one day they would regain their original value. Other things Harry sent home were of more value and beauty, including lovely china cups rescued from ruins and a small tapestry depicting a view of the Rialto Bridge in Venice, which Anne had framed. It graces her living room wall to this day.

Families all over America received such packages from the front in 1945, as the Allies moved on to Berlin. Some might call them "spoils of war," but to the soldiers who gathered them up from destroyed houses, they were souvenirs, a way of telling loved ones back home, "Look, we've come through, we're winning, we've fought our way across Europe to victory." There were certainly moments, however, when the soldiers' darker sentiments became painfully clear. Harry wrote in one letter to Anne, "In their homes are splendid icons, paintings of Christ and divine spectacles, in their hearts the hatred that is the only plausible cause for these generations of Hell on Earth. For their hypocrisy, one can only hate them and wish them nothing but the worst, in this world and the next. But don't let me speak of things like that."

On May 7, 1945, Germany signed an unconditional surrender at General Dwight D. Eisenhower's headquarters in Reims, France. Victory in Europe Day was celebrated on May 8, even as the war continued to rage in the Pacific. Many months passed before Harry could return home, because his ability to speak fluent German made him a valuable man. Not until January 1946 was he able to ship home to Brooklyn.

Harry wanted Anne to marry him, and that summer she went north to meet his family, staying with his sister in Pennsylvania, who was warm and welcoming, as were his other family members. But Anne still harbored doubts about spending her life with Harry. She had loved his letters and would treasure them always. She also loved him, but with the war over, she felt she had to think about the future, and she didn't quite believe that she and Harry belonged together. Her hesitance was partially a matter of their religions: Harry was Jewish and she was Christian. But more important, Anne felt a deep instinct that she tries to clarify now: "Somehow, I just *knew* it wasn't right. I can't really explain it. But I just knew that for Harry to lead a long and happy life, and for me to lead a happy life, our paths should separate."

Harry took a job at a small newspaper in Brooklyn, pursuing his longtime ambition, but then entered the burgeoning business of advertising. After graduation, Anne became an inspiring and much loved history teacher at Wake Forest high school. She continued to date a number of young men, one of whom was Frank Kennedy, who had fought in North Africa and then Italy, receiving a Legion of Merit for inspiring leadership and ingenuity in building a road he had reconnoitered under fire at Castellonarato. He was a staff engineer at North Carolina State University, a kind man of unassuming strength whom she liked a good deal. Her affection for him grew steadily, and in the autumn of 1948 she accepted his proposal of marriage.

Anne had continued to correspond with Harry during those years, though less often, and she wrote to tell him of her engagement. His reply started with a bit of humor: "Sorry to disappoint, but Truman is STILL the big surprise of the year." He added that he had known she would marry Frank when he visited her in September. "It will, of course, be impossible for me to see 'the last of Miss Hetrick'—but where your good church bells chime out the glad tidings, listen for the whisper of a sigh from the

Anne's mother's
house in Raleigh,
North Carolina,
where they hosted
so many Sunday
dinners.

A V-Mail letter
from Harry to
Anne's mother,
Ida B., addressed
with the First
Army APO from
New York, sent
March 25, 1945.

*A letter that Harry sent Anne from "somewhere in Germany" on February 12, 1945, which starts, "Dearest Adorable, How much longer can it last, darling—or me? It's impossible to write much any more—no place, no time, no lights, not even candles." He also mentions in this letter the "old German paper money" he is enclosing for her.*

*The "Sad Sack" cartoon Harry sent Anne for Christmas, 1944.*

*Christmas card sent by Harry to Anne from Holland that same season.*

*The Christmas card Harry sent to Anne depicting Hitler as a snowman, also from that same season.*

*Anne and the "other man" she chose to marry, Frank Kennedy, at a party in 1948.*

*The telegram of congratulations that Harry sent to Anne on her wedding day, December 18, 1948.*

FROM THE CONTINENT OF EUROPE - 1944

big, bad city of the North—and with that whisper will come all the fond hopes and best wishes for the noblest lady I have known. Always in all ways, Harry."

A wedding telegram from Harry read simply, "Luck," and she did not hear from him again for several years. In 1950 he married Iris Resnick, also from New York, and he reestablished contact with Anne. Every year, the Kennedys and the Greissmans exchanged Christmas cards with news of their growing families. Anne and Frank had three children and forty-nine years of a very happy marriage. Frank died in September 1997, after a long battle with Parkinson's disease. That Christmas, Anne received a card from Harry and Iris as usual, but a few days later, Iris telephoned to tell her that Harry had passed away. She told Anne that, among his treasures, he had always kept a picture of Anne Hetrick from the days when he had first known her.

Later, Anne would learn that Harry's wife and children had memorialized Harry's way with words on his tombstone. The inscription read, "He could make words sing." Anne found a way to memorialize him, too: She gave his hundreds of letters to the North Carolina Museum of History in Raleigh, providing an eloquent archive of the World War II experiences of a young man from Brooklyn who fell in love with a beautiful young woman from North Carolina. They had not spent their lives together, as Harry had wanted them to, yet they remain forever linked in ways that Anne Kennedy is happy to celebrate even now.

THE YOUNG MEN FROM THE NORTH *who trained at military bases in the South were usually treated exceptionally well.* Southern hospitality welcomed them into the towns and homes of Georgia, the Carolinas, and the rest of the Deep South with all the warmth and friendship that could be mustered. But a few pockets of lingering tension, passed down from the Civil War, could flare up unexpectedly. Here they added an additional degree of tension to an already high-strung wedding day.

*Miriam Clark and Lloyd Clark during the war.*
*The photograph of Lloyd is one he had taken while stationed in Ireland,*
*at Miriam's request, because she did not have a picture of him when*
*he left to go overseas. She says she wanted to be sure to have a picture*
*so that his child would know what he looked like in case*
*he didn't come back.*

# *Lloyd and Miriam*

## CLARK

When war broke out in Europe, Lloyd Clark was one of those Americans who knew that his country wouldn't be able to stay out of it in the long run, despite deep-seated isolationist sentiments throughout the country.

Lloyd grew up in Rockland, Maine, attended Phillips Academy at Andover, Massachusetts, and went on to MIT. For several years he worked at General Foods in Rochester, New York. But after Hitler occupied Denmark, Norway, and France, Lloyd volunteered for the army and in January 1941 was sent to Camp Stewart in Hinesville, Georgia, with the 209th Coast Artillery Regiment. He turned twenty-nine that month, and with war on the horizon, he was not actively looking for a wife, especially not one who was nearly ten years his junior. But when he met Macon native Miriam Elizabeth Bidez, just turning twenty, his feelings quickly changed.

By the fall of 1941, Lloyd, whom everyone called Larry, knew that he wanted to marry Mimi, as she was nicknamed. Given his old-school upbringing and their age difference, he first went to Mimi's father to ask for her hand. Mr. Bidez liked and admired Larry and gave his permission without hesitation. When he proposed to Mimi, Larry told her that she should carefully consider the fact that he was nearly ten years older, because it could make a difference in their lives at some point. But Mimi was very much in love, and she didn't hesitate to say yes. They planned to marry in the spring of 1942.

After a year in the army, Larry was far more aware than the general public of rumors about an early American entry into the war, and at the end of November 1941, he suggested that they move up the wedding date to December 13. Naturally, Mimi's mother was somewhat distraught at the short notice, but she and Mimi managed to pull everything together. Mimi says Larry often commented that had her mother been born a couple of generations later, she would have made a great CEO.

Sure enough, Larry's sense that war was imminent proved to be all too correct. Pearl Harbor was bombed on December 7. With America suddenly in the conflict, Larry's life became far more complicated, and it was difficult for him to get away from Camp Stewart. He and Mimi dreaded a dispatch to another base far away, or even overseas.

On their wedding day, Larry was due at the Bidez house at two o'clock, and the wedding was scheduled for three o'clock. But he didn't show up at the appointed time. By two-thirty Mimi's father and brother were out pacing the sidewalk in front of the house. A neighbor from across the street came over and actually said, "I told you not to let Mimi marry that Yankee!" Mimi says that Larry showed up a few minutes after the neighbor's remark, "and we were off on the most wonderful, romantic life I could imagine."

As the war raged on, and more and more soldiers showed up for training in the South, a great many more Yankee boys married southern girls, and those lingering tensions subsided as the country came together to meet the challenge of the day.

Attached to the Royal Artillery of the British North Africa Force, Larry served in the campaign in Tunisia against the formidable forces of General Erwin Rommel, the "Desert Fox," and subsequently in the southern Italian campaign. After his discharge from active duty, he served as an instructor in the U.S. Army reserve officer school, retiring in 1972 with the rank of lieutenant colonel.

His consecutive business careers as a plant and contract engineer with Maxwell House Coffee and Hunt-Wesson took Larry and Mimi and their two daughters around the country, from New York to Florida, Tennessee, California, and eventual retirement in Savannah, Georgia, a peripatetic life that Mimi thrived on, having inherited some of her mother's

Larry in front of
his tent at Camp
Stewart in 1941.
Every time it
rained, he
recalled, his cot
was flooded.

Mimi out shopping in June 1943.

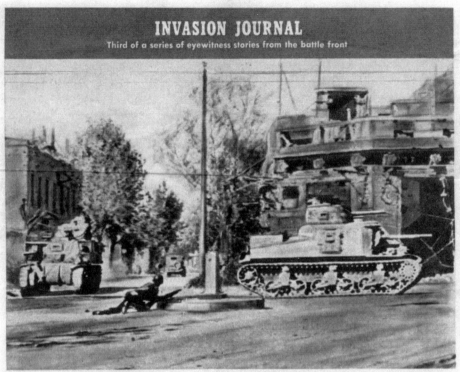

**INVASION JOURNAL**
Third of a series of eyewitness stories from the battle front

Two American tanks and a Yank move down a tree-lined street in Bizerte. The Grants ignore snipers, but the soldier is wary.

*A photograph from the October 5, 1943, issue of* Look. *The "Yank" mentioned in the caption is Larry.*

*Larry and Mimi, at the far left, out on the town with friends in 1945.*

*Larry and Mimi at their fifty-fifth anniversary party.*

remarkable organizational capabilities. "We started out from two completely different worlds," Mimi recalls, "and went on to explore a great many others together."

Their age difference was something Mimi never really noticed until Larry's death in 1997. "Now I understand what he was talking about," she says. "I miss him so very much."

DURING WORLD WAR II, MANY young couples found their sense of time warped by the circumstances. When a young man was about to be shipped overseas, he might feel as though he'd known a girl for months when he'd really met her a week before; the girl might feel that they had met just yesterday. While the young man was overseas, time could seem accelerated, so that when he returned to the States on leave and they could finally enjoy each other's company again for a bit, they might consider marriage. Should they marry right away, or perhaps the next time he got home; how long would that be? If they did marry, how would they calculate the time they'd known each other: add up the days and weeks since they met, or account only for the time actually spent together? Was it two years they'd been in love, or only two weeks?

*Charles and Patricia Lee in August 1945 after Charles
returned from thirteen months overseas.*

# Charles and Patricia
## LEE

Throughout their fifty-six years of marriage, Charles and Patricia Lee have been very much aware that if it hadn't been for World War II, they never would have met. Of course, the same could be said of many couples. But Patricia has developed a stronger feeling than most that "fate takes over your life." Indeed, there are elements of the Lees' story that suggest the hovering presence of fate more convincingly than usual.

At the high school Patricia Skinner attended while growing up in San Francisco, the year was broken into two semesters, one from September to January and the other from February to June, along with a summer-school term. Students were assigned to either a fall class or a spring class, and Patricia was in the fall class of 1941, scheduled to graduate in January 1942. At the graduation a month after the Pearl Harbor bombing, half the boys in her class were already in the armed services. The graduation was supposed to have been held at the beautiful San Francisco Opera House, but because of the citywide blackout ordered shortly after Pearl Harbor, the ceremony was held in the school auditorium instead.

Along with San Diego, San Francisco was the most important West Coast port of embarkation for ships heading out to fight the war in the Pacific. A sense of tumult and excitement permeated the city on the hills, and also a sense of danger. Early in the war, many feared that the Japanese would attack the West Coast of the United States, with San Francisco as a major target.

Many volunteer organizations in the city quickly established programs to help with the war effort and to offer solace to the young men from all across the country who were flooding the city, preparing to sail off to war. Patricia joined the Young Lady's Institute, which organized USO dances. At a Sunday-afternoon dance, a young man named Charles Lee walked over and asked Patricia to dance. She really liked this fresh-faced boy from West Rutland, Vermont, a seaman first class who was stationed at Treasure Island just offshore. Patricia says there was a strong physical attraction between them from the moment they saw each other. Not that she was about to give in to her feelings in any serious way—she was a properly raised young woman in a much more innocent time. She did spend the rest of that day with Charles (known as Chuck), showing him the sights. At the end of the evening, he asked to take her home. There was a general understanding among young women in those days about how to handle such an offer: You said that would be fine if the young man also took your girlfriends home. Any guy willing to do that was probably okay. Chuck said fine and excused himself briefly. Although Patricia didn't know it, he didn't have a penny, and he had to borrow a dollar from a fellow sailor in case he needed to pay for a streetcar or a jitney—cars that seated up to seven passengers. Chuck was so new to the city that he didn't even know what a ride cost—only a dime back then. He had to take three of Patricia's friends home that night, and she was suitably impressed.

After a week of seeing Patricia almost daily, Chuck asked her to go steady with him. But she didn't feel ready for that kind of commitment. Like so many other young women at the time, she had mixed feelings about getting seriously involved with a young man in the armed services; they arrived in port cities every day. While the supply of future husbands dwindled in small towns across America, parts of the country with major bases and ports swarmed with possibilities. Back in the small towns, young women tended to get married before their potential husbands shipped off to unknown destinies, but in the military boomtowns, women had good reason to wait and see who they might meet tomorrow—unless someone *very* special tumbled into their life. There was an unspoken sense that unless you were sure you had met the love of your life, you didn't need to rush into serious commitment.

Many young women had another concern: "Will I ever see him

again?" By the autumn of 1942, it was already clear that the war was going to be a long one, and that there were going to be great numbers of casualties. For young couples who were madly in love, that recognition fueled the desire to get married, or at least engaged, as soon as possible. But if either party felt doubt, the possibility that the young man might be heading off to his death often put a brake on an inclination toward marriage.

Patricia felt she simply did not know Chuck well enough even to say she would go steady. She had noticed among her friends and acquaintances that there were girls who would *say* they'd go steady but would start dating other young men soon after their "steady" was off at war. She didn't approve of that kind of behavior, and she didn't want to tempt herself to indulge in it. Better just to tell Chuck up front that as much as she liked him, she wasn't ready.

At the time Patricia met Chuck, he was a belly gunner in a torpedo bomber. That was a "top gun" kind of position, and Chuck was proud to have achieved it. But it was also perhaps the most dangerous job in the navy. The chances of survival as a belly gunner during the early stages of the Pacific war were close to zero.

One day shortly after Chuck had asked Patricia to go steady, he saw a notice on the bulletin board at Treasure Island that a new destroyer in port had just gone into service and needed men. This was an opportunity for him to switch out of his position as a belly gunner, and he signed up right away and shipped out on the destroyer to the South Pacific that very night. That decision almost surely saved his life. Every other belly gunner Chuck trained with was killed during the war.

After Chuck shipped out, he seemed to be gone from Patricia's life for good. He didn't write, which surprised her a little, even though she had refused to go steady. She wondered about him from time to time, whether he was all right. Though she'd dated quite a few other young men since Chuck left, none of them had been really special to her, and she regretted that they hadn't kept in touch. She asked a friend who worked at the Treasure Island base to see if there was any word of him. But the friend couldn't find his records, and Patricia was afraid he had been killed.

In September 1943, almost exactly a year since she had last seen Chuck, Patricia was pleasantly surprised by a telephone call from him. He was in port and asked if he could take her out that evening. She agreed, and they went to a movie. Chuck asked her for another date the next night, but then he didn't show. Patricia knew that this didn't necessarily mean she'd been stood up. His orders might have changed, and he might not have been able to get word to her. That happened frequently.

Still, she was surprised by the contents of a letter she soon received. Sure enough, Chuck was back at sea. But what stunned her was that he asked her to marry him. From a missed date to a proposal in one step was quite a leap. She wrote him a letter saying they'd discuss it next time he was on leave.

That was not until seven months later. Chuck got back into port on April 30, 1944, and they met again the next day. He proposed in person this time, and by now Patricia knew she was going to say yes. She was attracted to him in ways that went far beyond anything she had felt for anyone else. But even so, she made him wait a day before she accepted.

After all, she still didn't know him very well. In fact, when people soon began asking how long she had known him, she would say, "Two years," which was one kind of truth, though in terms of time she'd actually spent with Chuck, she had known him for only two weeks.

Both Patricia and Chuck were Catholic, which made them compatible in one sense but caused a problem in another. They knew that no priest would even think about marrying them for at least thirty days, and Chuck would probably be at sea again by then, although he did expect to be in port for a couple of weeks for repairs on his ship. They considered their options and decided to get married immediately, which they could do at city hall. This turned out to be much more of a saga than they expected.

Their plan was to meet at city hall on the morning of May 4, with Chuck and Patricia each bringing along a friend to serve as best man and bridesmaid. Patricia told her mother about the plan but said nothing to her more conservative father. He was a city inspector, and by an amazing coincidence, he happened to be working at the corner of Van Ness and Market Streets on the morning of the ceremony, very near city hall. Sure enough, Patricia's father looked up and noticed Chuck, whom he had met a couple of times, walking toward him, carrying a suitcase. He greeted Chuck and asked him where he was going. Chuck managed to stammer out that he was taking the suitcase to a friend who'd suddenly gotten leave. Patricia's father, totally unsuspecting, sent the nice young man on his way—to marry his daughter.

But that was just the beginning of the day's difficulties. According to California law at the time, the groom had to be twenty-one and the bride eighteen to marry without parental consent. The clerk at the courthouse asked them for identification. Patricia was nineteen and had no trouble with her identification, but when the clerk looked at Chuck's, he detected that the birthdate had been altered. Not to be thwarted, Chuck said he'd go get verification and dashed off to his ship, while Patricia waited, wondering how old Chuck really was.

After what seemed an eternity, Chuck rushed back in with a freshly signed paper from one of the officers on his ship. But all that it actually said was that he was serving in the navy and had seen combat in the South Pacific. The clerk read this over, looked at the expectant couple, read it again, and then, after what seemed like *another* eternity, he said, "Well, I'll accept this."

So Patricia and Chuck became Mr. and Mrs. Charles H. Lee on May 4, 1944. Exactly how old was Chuck that day? Like his bride, he was nineteen, but Patricia didn't find that out until after the wedding. Nor did she very much care.

Getting a hotel room on short notice in San Francisco in 1944 wasn't easy, but they were lucky, and they spent their first night together in real comfort. But then Chuck got the disappointing word that instead of remaining in San Francisco for repairs, his ship had received orders to undergo them in Hawaii, and he would be in town for just five more days. One of those would be taken up with the job of getting married all over again.

When Chuck and Patricia told her parents about the marriage—news only to her father, of course—they were determined that a traditional marriage service should be performed. Though a church wedding was definitely out, Patricia's mother pleaded with the priest at their church to perform the service, and because the couple was already legally married (if you didn't count Chuck's real age), he decided to make an exception for the special circumstances of the war. Chuck and Patricia were married once again in a small service in the priest's home.

During the following year, Chuck's destroyer, the U.S.S. *Lang*, DD-399, engaged in almost every major battle in the South Pacific, from Guam to Saipan to Leyte Gulf. Chuck wrote when he could find time, but his letters often took weeks, even months, to reach Patricia. All this time, she seldom knew in any detail where he was. All she really knew for sure was that the war in the Pacific was fierce and that he was in grave danger. Whenever he could, Chuck gave enough money to fellow sailors heading back to the States to buy Patricia a dozen roses, but not one of those bouquets ever got to her.

On April 12, 1945, Patricia was feeling particularly low. This was her twentieth birthday, and she hadn't heard from Chuck in months. To make a dismal day even darker, word suddenly came over the radio at the office of the hospital she worked in that President Roosevelt had died. Like many others, Patricia burst into tears. As was the case with offices all over the country, her office closed immediately. Roosevelt's death was a crushing blow to the country, and the world seemed an even more dangerous place with his passing. Few people realized at the time what good hands the country was in with newly sworn-in President Harry S. Truman.

Half a world away that April 12, Chuck was off the coast of Okinawa on "picket" duty: His ship formed part of the line of defense protecting the troops advancing on the beachhead. "We were suffering some of the worst kamikaze attacks of the war," Chuck would write years later. "I had just heard the sad news that President Roosevelt had passed away. It was my wife's birthday, and I had been gone for nearly a year. Some time before I had sent money with a shipmate who had been transferred off the ship to buy her red roses for her birthday. I was wondering if she had received the flowers. Then, above me, I saw a kamikaze headed straight for our ship. Our guns had damaged his controls, but I could even see the pilot's face as he tried to aim his plane at us. He missed the ship by only a few yards and crashed into the sea. I said a little prayer of thanks and at the same time wept for our departed president. It was the darkest day of the entire war for me."

But back in San Francisco, something life-affirming was happening. Remarkably, after so many failed efforts, Chuck's roses reached Patricia this time. When she got home early from her office that day, she discovered a box of twelve long-stemmed red roses at her door.

*Chuck and Patricia on their first date in September 1942 at the Lake Merced Rod and Gun Club picnic.*

*The ship Chuck served on, the U.S.S. Lang. His gun is the third from the left.*

*Chuck and Patricia on a cruise in 1996.*

Soon she began to receive letters from Chuck again. Okinawa had been taken, and Chuck promised to be home soon. She was expecting him to show up for his birthday, but he surprised her and arrived several days early, with no warning, on June 23. Even though Patricia says with a laugh that she was perturbed because she was having what is now called a "bad hair day," she couldn't remember ever being happier.

Charles and Patricia Lee have a son and a daughter who have done their parents proud. On May 4, 2000, the Lees celebrated the fifty-fifth anniversary of a very happy marriage between a sailor from rural Vermont and a big-city girl from San Francisco, who had known each other for two years that were really only two weeks when they wed in the spring of 1944.

FOR EVERY COUPLE WITH NO hesitations about running off on a moment's notice to get married, there was probably another couple in which one of the two had doubts. Sometimes those doubts didn't surface until the last minute. The woman might wonder if this was really the right man, or whether he would survive the war; what kind of future might they have together, since they really didn't know each other well at all. This could be the plot of any number of Hollywood movies made during the war. Such movies varied a great deal in quality, but even the most sentimental of them, now long forgotten, held audiences in those days because they dramatized a pressing issue. Real versions of these stories were happening all the time during the war, and some of them ended even more happily than any Hollywood script.

*Hank and Mary Jo Suerstedt in the summer of 1946 at the*
*New Orleans NAS Officers' Club.*

# Hank and Mary Jo
## SUERSTEDT

Mary Jo Bass grew up in Laredo, a small Texas town on the Mexican border. "My father was a dentist, and Mother was the typical housewife of that time. We weren't rich, but we were comfortable. New clothes for Easter, that kind of thing. But most important, looking back, was the fact that my sister, brother, myself, and Mom and Dad lived in a real house. Front yard, backyard, and neighbors stopping by all the time just to say hello. Being kids, we didn't know how lucky we were. And little did I know that I wouldn't live in a house of my own again for many years. 'Home' was destined to become a succession of navy quarters, rental houses, and even an apartment or two."

That destiny began to unfold at the end of 1942. Mary Jo, a young woman now, was dating a naval officer stationed in Corpus Christi. One day she received a phone call from another young officer, who delivered a farewell message from the officer she had been dating, who had to leave abruptly for duty in the South Pacific. "I thought it was very kind of the friend to take the trouble to call me. He was, after all, a total stranger. I asked him his name." His first name was ordinary enough—Hank. But the last name, Suerstedt, was unusual. "What kind of name was that, I wondered. It never entered my mind that I would end up carrying that name around for the rest of my life! The humorous part is that this young man was just pretending to pass along a message of farewell. He'd simply 'inherited' his friend's address book. We would laugh about that a lot over the years."

Mary Jo and Hank talked more, and she agreed to meet him, but they postponed the date when she came down with strep throat. They rescheduled for New Year's Eve, 1943. As things turned out, she got to meet him three days earlier, because he showed up at her home with a navy doctor to make sure she'd be well enough to celebrate. "Whatever that nice doctor did, it worked!"

But there was more to it than that. Mary Jo admits that on the basis of just a few phone calls and that one visit to her home, she was falling in love for the first time in her life. Pictures from that time reveal why they would be attracted to each other. Both Mary Jo Bass and Hank Suerstedt were physically dazzling enough to have been movie stars. Mary Jo had the classic beauty of a Loretta Young, while Hank had Gregory Peck's rugged appeal, except that he was blond.

New Year's Eve came, and Hank presented Mary Jo with a lei made of red carnations instead of the usual corsage. "Impressive, to say the least," Mary Jo recalls. "Our romance began at midnight with a kiss."

They saw each other every second Hank could be away from duty over the next eight months. Then the inevitable happened; Hank was called to the Pacific in September 1943. He asked Mary Jo to marry him, and she had gone so far as to pack her bags to accompany him to San Francisco, where she would wait for him as his wife.

Then the enormity of her decision settled in. "Was I brave enough? Did I love him enough? I went a little bit crazy." She faced the unspoken fear that she could be a wife for a very short time, then suddenly a war widow. At the very last minute, she changed her mind about accompanying him. They would wait and see what happened.

Hank Suerstedt reported for duty to a composite squadron made up of fighters and torpedo bombers. He was assigned to the latter group and, during the ensuing nine months, was involved in training exercises up and down the West Coast, from San Diego to Pasco, Washington. In July 1944 he was finally deployed on the U.S.S. *Marcus Island*, an escort carrier, and he fought in the Battle of Leyte Gulf that October.

"Somewhere along the line," Mary Jo remembers, "I think we both decided we had done the right thing in not marrying. We exchanged many letters, telegrams, even phone calls, but by the time he left for the South Pacific, it just seemed to be over between us. I don't have to tell you that wars do horrible things to people. I'm not apologizing for myself, but I was young and very confused."

Mary Jo's confusion did not last long, however. In March 1946, with the war well over, Hank had to make a trip to Corpus Christi on naval business, so he telegramed Mary Jo to suggest that they meet for coffee at the Driscoll Hotel. That meeting was all it took for both of them to realize all over again that they were made for each other. "'Soul mates' wasn't a term in use at the time," Mary Jo recalls, "but in retrospect, I believe our forty-four years together were proof that it was meant to be. At least I like to think so, for our true romance began with our marriage in April of 1946."

Mary Jo and Hank wasted no time in starting a family. Before long, their daughter Candace arrived, with Cynthia following three years later. Hank had been accepted into the regular navy shortly after the couple were married. He did two tours during the Korean War, three during the war in Vietnam, and five in Washington, rising to the rank of rear admiral and serving as deputy commander of naval operations in Southeast Asia during the latter years of the conflict in Vietnam.

"We moved twenty-three times in twenty-seven years," Mary Jo says with a grimace. "It wasn't easy, to say the least, to have a nomadic life, especially for the girls. I have to brag about our daughters. They just got used to being uprooted and transplanted time after time. Making new friends and then moving on. Both of our girls were pros from day one."

Mary Jo has held on to an anonymous article a friend sent her several years ago, which she feels accurately describes what a military wife must cope with. In the article, a conversation takes place between an angel and the Lord, after he had spent six overtime days working on his model for military wives. The angel wondered why the Lord was having so much trouble. Wouldn't the standard model do?

THE LORD REPLIED, *"Have you seen the specs on this order? She has to be completely independent, possess the qualities of both father and mother, be a perfect hostess to four or forty with an hour's notice, run on black coffee, handle every emergency imaginable without a manual, be able to carry on cheerfully, even if she is pregnant and has the flu, and she must be willing to move to a new location ten times in seventeen years.*

*Lieutenant Hank Suerstedt while serving in the Korean War from 1953 to 1954.*

*Hank being promoted to rear admiral on April 25, 1961, with Mary Jo at his side.*

*Hank and Mary Jo in the mid-1970s.*

*Mary Jo at home in the mid-1990s.*

*"And, oh yes, she must have six pairs of hands . . ."*

*After a considerable discussion of the problems involved, the angel noticed something strange on the cheek of the Lord's creation.*

*"There's a leak," the angel announced. "Something is wrong with the construction. I am not surprised that it has cracked. You are trying to put too much into this model."*

*The Lord appeared offended at the angel's lack of confidence. "What you see is not a leak," he said. "It is a tear."*

*"A tear? What is it there for?" asked the angel.*

*The Lord replied, "It's for joy, sadness, pain, disappointment, loneliness, pride, and a dedication to all the values that she and her husband hold dear."*

*"You are a genius!" exclaimed the angel.*

*The Lord looked puzzled and replied, "I didn't put it there."*

But while Mary Jo finds a good deal of wry truth in this piece, she is not about to complain. "I have to say that we had a front-row seat for history in the making. We joined the celebration in Hawaii when it became a state. We were in D.C. when President Kennedy was killed, and stood in the cold for hours to watch the funeral procession."

There were many other notable occasions through the years, and many pleasures of a quieter kind. "I can look back on an interesting and fulfilling life enhanced by wonderful friends, and blessings too numerous to count, though I continue to count them daily with thanks to God and Hank."

ILLIONS OF WOMEN WENT TO work in factories during the war, taking the place of men on assembly lines and building planes, tanks, and guns. *The first published photograph of Marilyn Monroe was taken in the California aircraft factory where she worked, by a photographer for the fabled GI newspaper* Stars and Stripes. *"Rosie the Riveter" became the national symbol for these women. Other adventurous women joined auxiliary branches of the armed services, the Waves, Wacs, and SPARS. The new sense of independence and of larger responsibility that these women found in their work spurred enormous social changes in postwar America.*

# *Mary Evelyn Porter*
## BERRY

Mary Porter grew up in Depression-era Arkansas. With the outbreak of World War II, she took a job in a defense plant that manufactured the pellets used to trigger the explosion of bombs. One day, she and a friend who traveled to the factory in the same carpool decided that they weren't really doing enough to help win the war, so they marched themselves down to a navy recruiting station to join up as Waves (Women Accepted for Volunteer Emergency Service) in May 1943.

Mary was sent to what she describes as a fairly "cushy" boot camp—Hunter College in New York City, where Waves from all over the country were given their basic naval training. Next she spent time in Norman, Oklahoma, training as an airplane mechanic, then was transferred to Millinton Air Force Base, in Tennessee, where she spent the rest of the war as an aviation machinist mate, third class.

Along with many of her coworkers, she was a bit disappointed not to be sent overseas, but her work refurbishing planes for operation on aircraft carriers did satisfy her desire to participate more directly in the war effort. She felt proud knowing that her work on aircraft engines was crucial to the safety of the American pilots.

In the spring of 1945, Mary got a new boss. His name was Gerald Grey Berry, machinist mate, first class. Previously he had served in the Pacific, stationed in Hawaii, and he had made a number of voyages to the South Pacific to work on planes damaged in the brutal battles to retake the Pacific islands. Gerry Berry transferred Mary from working on engines to patching wings. This new work involved a great deal of crawling around, but she liked it better because she didn't end each day covered in grease from head to toe.

Before long, Gerry and Mary started dating. The rules of courtship were quite different during World War II than they are today, when such a relationship would be prohibited in the military. Though she took plenty of ribbing from her coworkers—she was a hard worker and had formed many fast friendships with her fellow Waves long before Gerry arrived—she didn't run into any real animosity about her relationship with him.

Gerry and Mary dated for six months, and when they discovered they were due to be discharged simultaneously, they decided to get married on their last day in the navy. Dressed in their uniforms, with Mary wearing an orchid corsage, they went to downtown Memphis on December 15, 1945, to be wed by a minister in his office.

Both went to college on the GI Bill, and both also eventually took master's degrees. They had a son, whom they named Gary. Mary laughs about the family names. "Gerry Berry, Mary Berry, and Gary Berry—nobody who ever met us once ever quite forgot us."

Mary recalls with fondness the way Gerry would always tell the story of how they met. "I was washed over by a Wave," he would say. That good-natured joke hints at the profound social changes in relationships between men and women that the war put in motion. By joining the Waves, Mary became one of the pioneers in the evolution of the American armed forces as well as the creation of a vast range of new career opportunities for women.

In the years after the war, when Mary told people she had been in the navy, they always assumed she had been aboard a ship, and she always felt a little funny explaining that she spent the entire war in landlocked Tennessee. Though she had hoped and expected to be shipped overseas, she has never regretted in the slightest the work that she ended up doing. Not only did she play an important part in the war effort, she also met the man with whom she enjoyed fifty-four years of a wonderful marriage.

WHILE MANY WOMEN SERVED as mechanics in the armed forces, or as recruiting officers, the greatest need was for nurses. Young women just out of nursing school, as well as many more experienced nurses, suddenly found themselves in military uniform, tending to millions of soldiers and sailors at training camps across the nation, or to the wounded who were shipped back home from the front. These women were given officer rank, which not only signified their importance but also discouraged them from dating enlisted men, due to the "no fraternization" rules between officers and enlisted soldiers. Some couples, however, weren't about to be thwarted.

*Helen and Lowell Baker on their wedding day,
March 24, 1945. Helen was a second lieutenant and
Lowell a staff sergeant at the time.*

# *Lowell and Helen*

## BAKER

In May 1944, Lowell R. Baker was assigned to photo-mapping training with the army air force at Will Rogers Field near Oklahoma City. On the twenty-fourth, a cloudy, dreary day, he joined the regular crew of ten aboard a B-24, along with three ground personnel who needed to complete their flying hours for the month.

His plane was flying below cloud cover at an altitude of fifteen hundred to two thousand feet. Lowell was in the tail section, talking on the intercom with the pilot, when the plane made a simple regulation turn and suddenly the number-one engine, out of four, conked out. Moments later, to the crew's horror, both the number-two and number-three engines also died, and the pilot was left with very little control over the plane. He desperately tried to make it back to the base landing strip, but about a mile and a half short, the plane started diving down, heading toward a group of children picnicking in a schoolyard. The pilot banked sharply to the right to avoid them, then immediately banked sharply left to miss a barn across the street from the school. Now completely out of control, the plane took the top off of a huge mulberry tree as it crashed and catapulted across a field, wing over wing. The tail turret snapped off, and the five men in that section of the plane survived; the eight others were killed. An investigation showed that the plane had been filled with 91 octane instead of 100 octane fuel.

Helen Mondzak, a second lieutenant nurse assigned to the base hospital, heard sirens go off at around noon that day and knew there was trouble. Along with all the other off-duty nurses, she rushed to the hospital to lend a hand. Miraculously, two of the survivors were not badly injured, but the other three had suffered serious burns. Lowell was the one in the worst shape, with burns on his head, arms, and legs.

Helen was assigned to the ward in which all three men—Lowell, Roy Splawn, and George Connor—recuperated. Lowell was in critical condition in an oxygen tent, with his eyes bandaged. For days, he couldn't see the friendly woman who was caring for him. Later, during months of recuperation in the ward, where there was always lots of good-natured joking between the nurses and the men, he and Helen got to know each other well. Eventually, Lowell, Roy, and George were all released from the hospital, and they returned to training. "By that point in the war," Lowell recalls, "if you were breathing, they wanted you."

Not long after, Helen attended church with a friend one Sunday. Lowell and Roy were also attending that day, and they took seats right behind Helen and her friend. As part of the continual joking that went on in the hospital ward, Roy and George had regularly teased Lowell and Helen about getting married someday. As they all left church, Roy said to the two of them, "I didn't know it was going to be a church wedding." That evening, September 16, 1944, Helen and Lowell went on their first date. They remember the exact date because it happened to be Lowell's father's birthday.

They already knew each other so well that a serious relationship developed quickly. But because Helen was an officer and Lowell was a staff sergeant, they had to maneuver around the rules governing the behavior of officers and enlisted personnel. They couldn't be seen together in public places, so they met almost every weekend somewhere off the base, either at a friend's place in Oklahoma City, where they would have a meal and play cards, or at the home of Lowell's great-uncle Art and great-aunt Ina, who also lived in Oklahoma City.

Before long, they started talking about getting married, but in that "probably" and "eventually" way that was so common for many wartime couples. Then, in March 1945, Lowell got word that he would soon be sent to the western Pacific. One Saturday evening, Uncle Art asked Helen and Lowell what they were planning to do the following Saturday, and Lowell blurted out, "We're getting married."

Because Lowell was about to be sent overseas, the army air force looked the other way about the marriage, and also didn't inquire too closely into how the nurse and former patient had become prospective bride and groom.

Lowell and Helen were married by a Baptist preacher in Uncle Art and Aunt Ina's living room on March 24, 1945, and they spent a one-night honeymoon at a hotel in Oklahoma City. Three weeks later, Lowell left for the Pacific. That day he went to say good-bye to Helen at the ward, but then came back when his flight was delayed by fog. Before long the fog cleared, and just before his flight took off, he telephoned her to say one last good-bye. "It was hard enough saying good-bye," Helen remembers, "without saying it all day."

Lowell was assigned to the Fifty-fifth Weather Reconnaissance unit. They flew out of Guam, Iwo Jima, and Okinawa, and spent weeks flying reconnaissance for the B-29 bombers coming from the Mariana Islands on raids over Tokyo. As the U.S. forces planned a full-scale invasion of Japan to begin in November, President Truman approved the dropping of atomic bombs on Hiroshima and Nagasaki, on August 6 and 9, and the war came to an abrupt end.

Helen requested a discharge in October, which was granted, and she returned to her family home in New Jersey to await Lowell's return. They were reunited in Philadelphia on December 7, 1945. The nurse and patient who had once conspired to circumvent the rules could now fraternize in earnest: They had seven children who gave them eleven grandchildren and one great-grandchild. Helen says she feels they've been blessed to have fifty-six years of marriage. They now live happily in Austin, Minnesota.

*Helen at her desk at
Will Rogers Field
Base Hospital in
November 1944.*

*The ruins of
Lowell's plane
after it crashed.*

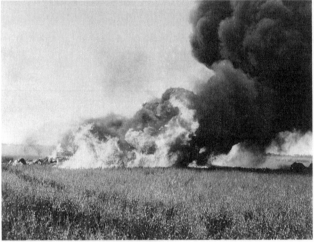

*The tree that the plane
crashed through, with
the number-two propeller
lying on the ground
in front. The plane
catapulted another
hundred yards and
landed in an oat field.*

*Newspaper article reporting the crash.*

*Top: The exit hole at the back of the plane where the survivors exited. Bottom: The remains of the plane after the fire was put out.*

*Lowell and Helen on their fiftieth wedding anniversary, in June 1995, with their seven children (top to bottom row, left to right): Bryan, Bryce, Blaine, Bradley, L. Robert, Loann, and Linda.*

EVEN IF A COUPLE SPENT SEVERAL
months getting to know each other, a decision
to get married could be driven by sudden
changes in circumstances. If both the man and the
woman were in uniform, the possibility of reassignment any time made long-term planning difficult,
and such orders sometimes led to spur-of-the-moment
weddings that resembled the plots of those wildly
popular prewar Hollywood screwball comedies.

*Eli and Bernice Fishpaw in 1944.*

# Eli and Bernice

## FISHPAW

Bernice Newton joined the Army Nurse Corps in September 1942. "I had just finished a postgraduate course in operating-room procedure," Bernice recalls, "and was eager to get into action." But her first assignment at Fort Wayne in Detroit, Michigan, proved disappointing. The military garrison was a huge ordnance depot, but at the time it consisted of little more than a detachment. The hospital had only twenty beds and was more like an infirmary. Surgeries were "limited and boring." So, Bernice explains, "I had no sooner been issued my old-style blue uniforms and learned to salute than I requested a new assignment to go overseas."

In mid-March 1943, Bernice was assigned to the 222nd Station Hospital, which was training at Fort Jackson, South Carolina. It was there that Bernice was really turned into an army officer. "The first six weeks we were taught how to drill. When a group is in formation and doing close-order drill, it brings them together better than any other experience I have ever had." The nurses also learned military law, procedure, and survival. The latter training included gas drill, which Bernice hated. "The gas chamber was a squad tent in which tear gas was released. We had to enter before we were allowed to don the mask—so that we could experience the gas and the protection we received from the gas. Some people threw up, but I held my breath and that didn't happen to me." They were also issued field equipment and taught how to erect pup tents, make bedrolls, prepare meals, and clean mess gear in the field. "One little glitch was that our fatigue suits were one-piece coveralls and did not have any accommodation for people who sit down to relieve themselves. This presented an interesting problem when using a straddle trench. Fortunately it was summertime, and hot."

During this rigorous training, Bernice met Eli Fishpaw, who was a member of the 100th Infantry Division, newly activated and training just down the road. "One day word was spread that there was a second lieutenant artillery officer who needed a date, but since he had hurt his knee playing football, he couldn't dance. I had never learned to dance myself, so this seemed the perfect date for me. When we were introduced, I misunderstood his name. I heard Eli Fishball instead of Fishpaw. I really thought someone was putting me on."

The nurses' quarters stood directly across the street from the number-two station hospital, and the hospital officers' club was used for the dance. The club was air-conditioned, which was unusual, so it was a good place to spend an evening. "Since we were not dancing, and I really didn't care to drink very much, we spent most of the evening talking. What did we talk about? Eli talked about his howitzers. Being a farm girl who had tagged along with my father, and knowing a lot about machinery, I was actually interested. So before the evening was over, Eli had invited me to come to the gun park and see his howitzers. I don't think he actually expected me to do that, though. The next day, when I was walking down the road toward the 374th Field Artillery area where they were training, he saw me coming and quickly gave the order to close up the guns and knock off for the day. He hopped into a jeep and drove down the road to meet me. He asked me if I would like a ride in his jeep. Strangely enough, the ride took me straight back to the nurses' quarters."

Bernice and Eli continued to see each other all that summer. Eli even let Bernice borrow his car when he was out in the field. "I would tell the nurses that if they would get some gas ration coupons, we could go to one of the lakes on the post and have a swim." It wasn't difficult to collect coupons from the hospitalized soldiers, because the coupons usually expired before they were well. "So even though the car had twelve cylinders, we always had plenty of gas. This suited Eli, since the tank was often full when he returned to camp to reclaim his thirsty car."

Bernice continues, "By the end of the summer, Eli and I—or anyway,

I—had decided we should get married." The division was scheduled to go on maneuvers in December, and the 222nd had left for the Pacific without the nurses. Bernice felt in limbo. "One Saturday in November, Eli and I drove to Camden in the next county and purchased a marriage license. We could have been married there, but I thought it would be nice to get married by a chaplain, so we headed back to the post. But on the way we had to pass the University of South Carolina football stadium, and there was a game in progress, so we decided to wait until the next week to get married and went to the game instead."

While they waited out the week's postponement, they planned "to get a little fancy and invite the 374th officers and the 222nd nurses and leave the church under an arch of howitzers." Bernice even rented a small apartment off-post. "But the best of plans can go astray. On Tuesday, the 222nd nurses received orders. Were we going to join our hospital unit in the Pacific? No. We were to proceed to Camp Forrest, in Tennessee, to be the cadre for the 216th General Hospital unit. By our wedding day on Saturday, I was on the train to Tennessee."

But Bernice and Eli must have been destined to marry. Remarkably, shortly after Bernice left, Eli's 100th Division was assigned to Tennessee for maneuvers. "This made it possible for us to see each other on weekends. Eli has always insisted that he came to see me just to get a warm hotel room, but it might be pointed out that there were probably better rooms and more activities available for military men in Nashville than in Tullahoma."

Even if he had shown up only for the warm room, Eli and Bernice agreed once again to get married, in December. Because the courthouses were closed on weekends and Eli couldn't get away during the week, Bernice had to get the license. "Eli had the battalion surgeon give him a letter certifying that he was free of venereal disease, while I had the appropriate tests done on post and took the bus to Manchester, the county seat, to get the marriage license. However, the clerk would not issue this important document, because she could not accept Eli's letter." Fortunately, as was well known, the neighboring state of Georgia didn't require certificates of health to get a marriage license. And there was a small town—Rossville, Georgia—just over the state line that had a good reputation as a weekend marrying spot. Bernice and Eli decided to get married in Rossville on Saturday, January 1, 1944.

Surgery personnel who took calls on New Year's Eve could have the entire next day off, so Bernice volunteered. "It turned out to be an unusually busy night. The weather was at its worst, with a sleet storm in the mountains. We had five jeep accidents to worry about, most of them serious. This was very stressful for me, as I thought Eli was on the road traveling to Tullahoma. I had absolutely no sleep. The place was still jumping at seven in the morning, and I had not heard from Eli, so I continued to work until about ten, when I gave up and went to quarters and to bed thinking I had been stood up."

But at about noon, Bernice was wakened and told she had a phone call. "It was Eli. He had not been able to leave the battery the night before because all the other officers had departed and he was the only one left and had to stay. I caught the shuttle bus into town and met him at the King Hotel. He had had all the driving he wanted for that day, so we took a bus to Chattanooga. It was a very busy travel day, and the bus company had put on an extra bus that was old and tired. The driver was also the company mechanic, which I found somewhat reassuring. We left Tullahoma about three in the afternoon, heading into the storm and the mountains, where the roads got higher and narrower as we approached Chattanooga. The ancient bus would shift into low and, when I thought it was about to stall, would go into a still lower gear and chug on. It seemed to have an endless number of low gears. After getting to the top of each tortuous mountain, going down became much more exciting, as the bus preferred to do it sideways."

They finally arrived in Chattanooga about eight o'clock that night, with no idea of what to do next. "We found a taxi driver with an old-fashioned wooden leg who knew all about Rossville and 'Marrying Sam,' the character from the *Lil' Abner* comic strip. He drove us out to the Rossville city hall and accompanied us upstairs, where the mayor/justice of the peace was doing a thriving business. When it was our turn, our driver served as our witness. The ceremony, though short, was not totally meaningless as 'Hizzoner' read and we repeated the traditional vows. Eli tipped the driver twenty dollars."

The newlyweds decided to take the train back to Tullahoma. "We had a steak dinner—the steak was tough—with some wine in a restaurant at the train station. No cake. We caught the northbound train around midnight. It was packed. The coach we boarded was jammed with sailors returning to Great Lakes, near Chicago, from furloughs. There were sleeping sailors in the seats, sleeping sailors on the floor, even sleeping sailors in the overhead racks. The only place we could find to stand was on the platform between the cars. Even this was crowded. There must have been six or seven people who had just come aboard. One was an older lady, and she was given a duffel bag to sit on. While I was cold and tired after having worked twenty-seven hours, plus the stress of the day, I was too numb to care. Only when we went through a tunnel did we notice the inconvenience—we were showered with coal smoke."

Back in Tullahoma, Bernice and Eli made their way to the King Hotel, where he had rented a room on the fourth floor. "As we were climbing the stairs, I met an officer who was dating one of the nurses from the 222nd. I was embarrassed to be caught in a sleazy hotel at four in the morning and wasted no time announcing that we were married, even flashing our new certificate to prove it. But there were chores to be done before we could fall into bed. It was raining, and the ceiling was dripping water. This was solved when we found an old-fashioned chamber pot in the closet. There was a real bathroom, too. Eli decided he wanted to wash his underwear and fatigues, which we did in the bathtub, stomping them primitive-style with our feet and then spreading them on the radiator to dry. I didn't have to report for duty until noon, and Eli had to be back at the battery the following morning.

"And that," Bernice says, "is the story of how I met and married my husband of fifty-six years, Eli Fishpaw." She and Eli have recounted this and other adventures in a charming self-published book titled *The Shavetail and the Army Nurse: The Bride Wore Olive Drab.*

THE GREAT PORT CITIES OF
America, from New York to San Francisco
and San Diego to Norfolk, were bustling
hubs of World War II activity, and no port was closer
to the war than Hawaii's Pearl Harbor. Due to its
strategic importance as the major staging point for
the Pacific war, there was a special intensity to life
there, and important visitors showed up regularly,
though not always with any warning.

*James and Virginia Cowart in 1944,*
*just before he left for sea duty.*

# James and Virginia
## COWART

Virginia Melville grew up in Hawaii, where her father, who had fought in World War I, took a shipbuilding job after retiring from the navy in 1934. In the spring of 1942, Virginia temporarily dropped out of high school to participate in the war effort as a civilian employee in the Registered Publications Issuing Office. That November, several new young naval officers were assigned to her office. They were nicknamed "ninety-day wonders," referring to their accelerated three-month training courses. One of these young officers was Ensign James Cowart, and it didn't take long for Virginia to realize that "Mr. Cowart" had taken more than a casual interest in her.

"I ignored it," Virginia says. "I had never dated an officer. I assumed that they were staid and constrained. Was it because my father was a retired navy chief? I don't know, but I commented to a friend, 'I don't think they're as much fun as enlisted men.' It was unfair of me to form such a biased opinion, and I found out later that I was wrong."

One day, Ensign Cowart said to her, "I'd like to take you out, but I don't have a car. I wouldn't want to take a girl on a bus." Again, Virginia ignored the advance, and another day, when he repeated his comment about the bus, she decided he wasn't interested after all. What was so bad about taking the bus? He must just be using that as an excuse, she reasoned: "Huh, I have to ride the bus every day." In any case, Virginia was never at a loss for dates: In wartime Hawaii, women were far outnumbered by men.

A while later, Virginia returned to high school so she could graduate with the classmates she had known since the second grade. Like her, many had temporarily put their education aside to help in the war effort. Others had evacuated to the States, frightened of Hawaii's vulnerability. Many of the young men from her class were now in the military. In fact, Virginia's class size had decreased from 1,330 to 717 pupils. Still, she was glad to have the chance to finish high school with the promise of the job at Pearl Harbor after graduation. The job itself—correcting secret, confidential, and restricted coded publications sent out to the American and British Pacific fleet—made her feel she was doing something significant.

When she returned to her job at the Issuing Office after graduation, there was Ensign Cowart working in the front office along with several other young officers and enlisted men she had known from before. They gave her a hearty welcome, and Jim Cowart seemed especially glad to see her. Maybe he was interested after all?

For Virginia's nineteenth birthday in August 1943, a close friend collaborated with Virginia's parents to throw her a surprise party. Ensign Cowart was among the fifteen or so invited guests, and when it came time for Virginia to open her presents, he took her aside and told her that he would like to give her his present privately.

As they walked outside into the darkness of the standard regulation blackout, lit only by a partial moon, Virginia remembers thinking, "Uh-oh, what is he up to?" On the way out, they passed Virginia's parents and her sister in the kitchen, who gave them a puzzled look. When she opened the gift, she was overwhelmed to receive something so valuable from this young man whom she had never even dated. In the box was a beautiful cultured pearl necklace, which he promptly placed around her neck. She stammered an embarrassed thanks, and when they went back into the house, she felt the blood rush to her face as her family looked at her in wonderment. "I detected the 'hmmmm' in my mother's eyes," Virginia says, laughing.

About a month later, Ensign Cowart finally asked Virginia for a date. "He furnished some gas ration coupons so that he could borrow my father's car for a ride to Blow Hole and Waimanalo before having dinner at the Halekulani Hotel, where he presented me with a beautiful orchid corsage and intimated that he would love to be the first to take me to the

States. I had told him that I was only three when my family left Coronado, California, and that I didn't remember it at all. So he now told me about all the places he wanted me to see.

"After dinner we saw *Hello, Frisco, Hello,* with Alice Faye and John Payne, at the Waikiki Theater. We arrived home before dark and the start of curfew. Jim asked if he could kiss me. That 'old-fashioned girl' feeling came over me. I shudder now when I think of my reply. 'But I hardly know you, Mr. Cowart.' It sounded like a line from a movie!"

This was not a line Virginia would ever use again. "Those World War II navy officers worked fast," Virginia says with a chuckle. "We became engaged two dates later. I guess he had to live up to the title of 'ninety-day wonder.'"

Now that they were a couple, the mystery of the bus excuse was revealed. Jim finally resorted to taking Virginia on the bus for some of their dates, and he explained that he had been reluctant before because he'd worried that enlisted passengers would make remarks. Officers with dates on buses weren't exactly a common sight.

Though their courtship was very fast, they took their time planning the wedding, and Virginia Melville and Ensign James Cowart were married on July 19, 1944.

Virginia vividly remembers an incident about a week after their wedding that combined a patriotic thrill, high-stakes presidential diplomacy, and domestic comedy. At that time, General Douglas MacArthur and Admiral Chester Nimitz were locked in a dispute about how the war in the Pacific should proceed. MacArthur was in a strong position at the time, because he had directed the campaign to retake New Guinea—which was just coming to an end—with strategic brilliance. He favored retaking the Philippines, thereby making good on his famous promise, "I shall return." Admiral Nimitz, however, backed by the Joint Chiefs of Staff, wanted to bypass the Philippines and move on to capture Formosa. The dispute had become so tense that President Roosevelt flew to Hawaii to meet jointly with MacArthur and Nimitz. MacArthur disliked Roosevelt, both personally and politically, and the president well knew it, but this was an election year, and he agreed with MacArthur that Americans felt a moral obligation to the people of the Philippines. It took him a month to convince Nimitz and the Joint Chiefs to go along.

Virginia and Jim were having dinner with her parents during Roosevelt's visit to Hawaii when they heard sirens. "It was unlike the usual police siren," Virginia recalls. "It sounded more like a parade motorcade. That was it! I had heard that the president was in Hawaii to confer with top military officers. 'It's President Roosevelt!' I shouted excitedly. 'Hurry!' We all jumped up from the table and ran outside—Mom, Dad, my sister Betty, Jim, and I. The president of the United States was headed in our direction—right past 3828 Pake Avenue, the home of the Melville family. As he passed us in his shiny black open convertible—which would never be done now—less than fifteen feet away, he waved enthusiastically. 'Hi, President Roosevelt,' we shouted. He smiled, waved back, and returned our greetings. That moment was ours to share and remember always. The president of the United States had interacted with us alone. I had seen him when he made previous visits to Hawaii, but we were always in a crowd. When he waved then, it was to scores of people. This day no one else was around."

As they walked back to the house, Virginia's mother began laughing. "Look at Jim!" she cried. They all turned and saw that Jim still had his napkin tucked into the pants of his khaki uniform. "I'll bet that no one has ever greeted the president of the United States with a uniform like this," Jim chortled, looking down at himself.

Jim was sent to sea soon thereafter and missed his new wife terribly. He was comforted not only by her picture, which he kept in his locker aboard the U.S.S. *Pennsylvania,* but by several other vivid reminders of her that kept cropping up. As communications officer, he went over any coded publications, which were constantly being updated back at Pearl Harbor. Virginia, of course, was one of the people doing that job, and whenever she made a change, she had to initial it. Jim wrote to her, "I was surprised to discover that the general Signal Book I was using had been corrected by none other than 'VEM.' I told some of my shipmates about it and they were impressed. Since then I've come across your initials numerous times in various publications. Other than your beautiful picture, it's the next best thing to having you right here with me."

Virginia recalls, "I was extremely proud of the fact that publications I had corrected were being distributed throughout ships and shore bases in the Pacific. *My* publications were being referred to by U.S. and British

*Right: Ensign James Cowart in November 1942. Below: Virginia Melville Cowart at age nineteen. Jim kept this photograph of her in his locker aboard ship.*

TERRITORY OF HAWAII
CITY AND COUNTY
OF HONOLULU

NON-RESIDENT OPERATOR'S

PERMIT NO.   43079

This is to certify that the person named and described below was issued a permit by the Examiner of Chauffeurs of the City and County of Honolulu, as a.......AUTO GAS..........Operator only under the provisions of Act 234, Session Laws of Hawaii 1937, for a period of 90-days from....8-23-43

NAME....COWART Jas. Wm. Jr. LT. (jg.)

RESIDENCE ADDRESS....USNR

LICENSE NO....M 17073.......STATE....Cal

NON-RENEWABLE

Licensee must sign here in ink

Sgt J Ornellas
Examiner of Chauffeurs
City and County of Honolulu

*Above: The driver's permit that Jim received just before his first date with Virginia, which allowed him to take her out in style instead of taking the bus. Right: The ticket stub from* Hello, Frisco, Hello, *the movie Jim and Virginia saw on their first date.*

*Jim and Virginia on their wedding day, July 19, 1944, in front of the Melville home in Honolulu, and their bridesmaids: Virginia's sister, Betty Ann (far right), Marian Kleinschmidt (next to Jim), and Barbara Donnell (next to Virginia).*

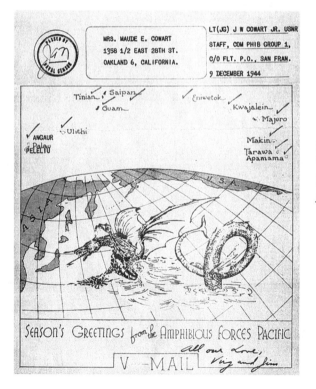

*V–Mail Christmas "card" from Jim and Virginia to his mother, sent December 9, 1944.*

THIS CERTIFIES THAT

*Virginia E. Melville*
(VOID IF NOT SIGNED)

IS HEREBY AUTHORIZED TO WEAR THE NAVY "E" LAPEL BUTTON IN RECOGNITION OF MERITORIOUS WORK PERFORMED AS AN EMPLOYEE OF THE

*U.S. Navy, Pearl Harbor* COMPANY. PART OF
(FILL IN NAME)

THE BATTLE OF PRODUCTION IS BEING WON THROUGH YOUR EFFORTS AND THIS "E" BUTTON IS VISIBLE PROOF OF THE NAVY'S RECOGNITION OF YOUR ACCOMPLISHMENT. WEAR IT ALWAYS.

DATE *11/2/42*          (SIGNED) *Frank Knox*
                        SECRETARY OF THE NAVY

*The certificate Virginia received for her work during the war.*

*Jim and Virginia with their first child, daughter Shirley Ann, born on October 2, 1945, in the Chelsea Naval Hospital in Chelsea, Massachusetts.*

*Jim and Virginia on a trip to one of their favorite places, Honolulu, Hawaii, in 1988.*

officers. The man I had married was using them on the U.S.S. *Pennsylvania* and wherever his duties took him."

James and Virginia Cowart have been married for fifty-six years and have two children and one granddaughter. (Unfortunately, they lost a grandson when he was twenty-four). "Jim kept his promise," Virginia says, "and showed me not only the States but the world. We settled in California, but Hawaii will always be home to me, and we return often for reunions, anniversaries, and vacations. We have Pearl Harbor and World War II to thank for bringing us together."

THE NONFRATERNIZATION RULES *designed to prevent officers and enlisted personnel from romantic involvement were applied very strictly on some bases, while on others, the senior officers looked the other way. There were also certain anomalies at work. While in training to become an officer, a young man could usually get away with dating an enlisted woman, particularly one in a different branch of the service. But once he was commissioned as an officer, the rules changed, and the resulting difficulties were sometimes comical, if not descending into outright farce.*

*John Darr when he was an aviation cadet, in early 1944.*
*Angeline Brown Darr, yeoman second class, in 1943.*

# John and Angeline

## DARR

In late 1943, John W. Darr was attending precadet training at the Army Aviation School of the Central Washington College of Education in Ellensburg, Washington. On Christmas, the students were given the day off. John and a friend were walking downtown that morning when they ran into a classmate and his girlfriend, who lived in town. She was having a party that night for friends who were home for the holidays, and because she was short of men, she asked John and his friend to come. They happily agreed.

At the party, John made particular note of the arrival of two very attractive Waves: a local girl and her roommate from Colorado. He found out later that they were both yeomen, stationed in Seattle at the Thirteenth Naval District Headquarters.

After some lively socializing, the entire party repaired to the local American Legion hall, where they spent the rest of the evening dancing and swapping life stories. John, by "great good fortune," selected Angeline Brown, the Wave from Greeley, Colorado, as his "date" for the evening. He had spent much of his youth on an Iowa farm and was fascinated by Angeline's very different background.

As their evening drew to a close, he asked his new friend for her address and promised to write to her. He knew another date anytime soon would be impossible; his outfit was just about to ship out to Santa Ana, California, for preflight training.

Over the next few months, John recalls, "a vigorous courtship evolved via the mails, during which—contrary to all logic—we agreed to marry just as soon as I graduated from aviation cadet training. Summertime found me at Victorville Army Air Field, training to become a bombardier. As luck would have it, I became hospitalized. Upon learning of this, Angeline was granted leave to come to visit me."

John was released from the hospital while Angeline was there, and they were sorely tempted to get married right away. But they decided to be sensible and wait for his graduation.

"Graduation took place on Victorville's hot desert sands on Saturday morning, October 28, 1944," John recalls. Their wedding was scheduled for seven-thirty the following evening in Seattle's Prospect Congregational Church. "Both our mothers were in attendance," John relates, "plus a large contingent of U.S. Navy personnel. First among them was Captain Howard Berry, the fine old gentleman for whom Angeline served as yeoman and personal secretary. Because Angeline's father owned a large and very successful restaurant back in Greeley, and there was such a shortage of help during the war, it was impossible for him to take the time off to attend the wedding. So Captain Berry brought her down the aisle and 'gave her away.' Unfortunately, the navy could afford to do without Angeline's services for only a single day. Our honeymoon, therefore, took place at the famous and luxurious Olympic Hotel, today's Four Seasons, in downtown Seattle. The next morning's paper carried a small story about the wedding that appeared under the pithy headline 'Army-Navy Merger.'"

Then it was back to duty for them both. Angeline continued as secretary to the director of personnel, Captain Berry, until the war's end. John's duties took him first to Tonopah, Nevada, and then to Langley Field, Virginia, where he was trained in the B-24 Liberator bomber.

While John was at Tonopah, Angeline arrived for a week's visit. The base commander had instituted a strict nonfraternization policy between officers and enlisted personnel. There was also a regulation against military personnel wearing civilian clothing at any time, since material was difficult to procure. "These factors," John recalls, "combined to provide a few rather exciting moments as Angeline and I shared drinks with another couple at the Tonopah Club one evening.

"As might be expected, she was attired in her navy yeoman first class uniform, while I was obviously an army officer. A clear violation of the rules! Two military policemen discovered us together and promptly placed me under arrest. I explained (or was it complained?) that this young lady beside me was—'Believe me, Sergeant'—my wife. They were not convinced and took me into custody. Finally someone back at the air field was rousted out of bed to check my personnel records, where they found that, *indeed,* my wife was, *in fact,* an enlisted member of the U.S. Navy, and I was released from custody. Until proven otherwise, I claim to be the only person ever arrested for having been seen in public with his wife."

At the war's end, Angeline and John rejoined in Colorado, where he enrolled at the University of Colorado. Their first son, George, was born there in the summer of 1947. A second son, Steven, was born in 1952. John and Angeline now have four grandchildren and one great-grandchild.

"Angeline and I often reflect on our happenstance meeting, realizing that the odds against our having a satisfactory marriage were tremendous. But we've met and beaten those odds! We've done so, we believe, for a number of reasons: We take our obligations seriously, we try to be honest with ourselves and others, and we have both been endowed with a damning conscience. We love and respect each other greatly as we face the future from the perspective of these 'golden years.'"

*Angeline and John on the day of their wedding in 1944.*

*Two "broken heart" pins, which John and Angeline bought before their wedding. Each of them wore one, out of sight under a lapel, until they were back together for good after the war.*

*Left: The army air force shoulder patch, in bullion as opposed to the more common plain cloth design. Right: The navy Waves collar insignia pin.*

*Angeline and John on their fiftieth wedding anniversary in 1994.*

For MEMBERS OF THE ARMED services who left sweethearts or wives at home, or who had fallen in love in one part of the world only to be yanked suddenly to another, one of the primary obstacles was wartime transportation. No matter the mode—car, bus, train, or plane—all you could really count on was a problem. With cars, you had to scrape together enough ration coupons to buy gas. Buses always ran late. Trains were jammed. And your seat on an airplane could be commandeered by someone of higher rank. But young lovers found ways to get together, even if their trip required an unscheduled stop in the middle of nowhere.

*Louis Funderburg in 1944 and*
*Judy Underwood Funderburg in October 1944.*

# *Louis and Judy*
## FUNDERBURG

Judy Underwood and Louis Funderburg had their first date in 1942, when she was still a high school student in Nashville, Arkansas. Louis had graduated from the same school the year before and was working at a defense plant in Texarkana, Texas. They dated for a while before Louis joined the navy, and they kept in touch by letter after he left. But their relationship was not exclusive. Judy dated other young men, and one day she wrote him a Dear John letter to say that she thought she would be marrying another man. As she recalls, "When I wrote him that letter, he came unglued. He wrote back and told me I had better forget that guy because *he* was the one I was going to marry." After several more persuasive letters, he won Judy over, and they became engaged by letter. Louis wrote to her that he would give her a ring when he could put it on her finger.

By early December 1944, Louis had been in the navy for two years. For the past year he had been serving on an oil tanker, shuttling oil from Aruba and Curacao in the Gulf of Mexico, through the Panama Canal to New Guinea and Darwin, Australia. He had served enough time to be eligible for a thirty-day leave, and while his ship was anchored at the canal, his commanding officer managed to find a replacement for him and get him the leave. Louis hoped he could get home to spend the Christmas holiday with his family. He and two other shipmates with leave left the ship, which was docked on the Pacific side of the canal. Their navy unit had a base in New Orleans, and they expected they would be transported there to get their leave papers. But they had no such luck.

Instead, they were sent on the Panama railway to a small naval base on the Caribbean side of the canal. There they waited for three days, checking constantly about their transportation to the States. Finally, a soldier found them and told them to follow him. They thought they'd be getting on a plane to New Orleans but were shocked to find they were being led to an LST [landing ship, tank] ship, a transportation ship for tanks that was heading for San Pedro, California. The first thing the ship did was pass through the canal, back to the side Louis and his friends had just come from, which took another whole day.

Once through the canal, Louis and the others had to help load supplies and fuel, and then they were finally on their way to the States. As luck—or their lack of it—would have it, a terrible storm hit the ship off the coast of Central America. An LST was not made for riding out such storms, and some of the crew even joked, "Let's open the doors [doors at the front of the vessel that swung open to unload tanks on beaches] and sink so we can get survivor's leave." To make matters even worse, one of the crew suffered an attack of appendicitis, and the LST had to steam to a port in Guatemala to get him medical care.

Finally, after twenty-one days on the LST, they reached San Pedro. Louis quickly looked into transportation from there and realized he would not quite be able to make it home for Christmas. He sent a telegram to Judy, asking her to meet him the day after Christmas in Texarkana. Because Texarkana bordered four states and hosted a large military base, it was a busy crossroads for thousands of men in all branches of the service. Louis decided to hitchhike to Texarkana, which was usually faster than taking buses during the war years, and almost any traveler would give a lift to a man in uniform.

He made such good time that he arrived way ahead of schedule, and rather than just wait around for Judy to arrive, he decided to take a bus to Arkansas. According to the schedule, he would arrive well before Judy left.

But the bus fell further and further behind schedule as the trip wore on, and by the time Louis got to Arkansas, he realized he had a problem. Judy had surely left for Texas—they would end up passing each other somewhere along the highway! He went up front and explained his plight to the driver. They were traveling along Highway 71 near Ashtown, Arkansas, and Louis calculated that if they could stop in Ashtown, the timing should be right to catch Judy's bus stopping there on its way west. Though this sounded like a good plan, the driver said that the stop for Ashtown was outside of town, on the highway, and he didn't think Judy's westbound bus would necessarily be stopping there. But he agreed to stop and try to flag down Judy's bus as it went by.

Sure enough, the bus from Nashville soon pulled into sight, and the driver put his arm out the window to hail it. The bus came to a stop, and Louis's driver called across to ask if there was a Judy Underwood on board. Sitting halfway back, Judy was startled when her driver called out her name, and cried out, "Yes, I'm here!" She rushed to the front of the bus, while Louis hopped off of his, and they bolted toward each other, meeting in the middle of Highway 71, where they embraced passionately to the loud cheers and whistles of the passengers aboard both buses.

Louis and Judy had decided that they would put off their wedding until he was out of the service, but their ardent reunion in the middle of Highway 71 prompted them to tie the knot right away. They climbed aboard the bus Louis had been traveling on, returned to Nashville, and were married at the home of a friend on New Year's Day, 1945.

Louis returned to his ship when his thirty-day leave ended. Judy had no idea how long it would be before she would see him again. Then, in early August of 1945, Louis's ship came into port briefly at Oakland, California, just north of San Francisco, and he cabled for Judy to come and visit. His ship was scheduled to return to sea on August 15, so after a wonderful but all too short visit, Judy returned to Arkansas on August 14, which turned out to be Victory in Japan Day. That afternoon, Louis heard the report that Emperor Hirohito had announced Japan's surrender in a radio broadcast. All aboard ship had been granted liberty until nine the next morning, and Louis decided to head to downtown San Francisco to take part in the huge celebration he was sure would be going on.

Louis wrote Judy a letter describing the celebration vividly:

Well, I couldn't resist going to Frisco. I know Frisco would celebrate in an all-out fashion. At first I wondered if I had done the right thing

*Louis and his friend Glen
Broomfield before they left
Panama in November 1944.*

*Louis aboard the
LST that took him
on his circuitous
journey from
Panama to
San Pedro.*

The cover of a coupon book issued to Louis for commissary meals at the Panama Canal.

Louis and Judy in 1944.

Louis and Judy at home, Christmas 2000.

or not, because from what I saw in Oakland, it was getting pretty rough. I could hardly believe my eyes. Most of the service men were kissing any woman they could get their hands on. Everyone was exchanging hats and clothes, and you might think it was a panic. . . . I wish you could have been with me, but still it wouldn't have been safe for you, because I know I wouldn't have stood for all those guys kissing you. . . . Some was the fault of the women, because I saw lots of them go up and kiss service men who weren't even drinking. . . . I walked to First and Market and the people had completely taken over Market Street. . . . The streetcar rail-guards had been broken off and every few feet I was stumbling over them or boxes and signs. . . . fire crackers were going off—some sounded like bombs. I was afraid one might land too close for comfort and later a few did come pretty close. . . . I walked down close to Fifth and there was a big bonfire in the middle of the street. They were burning everything they could find—War Bond booths, paper stands and flower stands. Almost everyone had a bottle, most of them partially gone. I saw one sailor drop a bottle almost full. He and his buddy were standing there weeping over it as if it were his dead mother. . . . People were climbing the tallest buildings—to the tenth and fifteenth stories. The statue of Franklin, close to Market and Stockton streets, was climbed, too. A Marine stood on top, holding a flag. . . . I took refuge in a USO to have a cup of coffee. There were plenty of drunks there—the celebration was in full session in the USO. There was a room for enlisted men and one for officers who had passed out, and they were stacking them up—loaded to the gills. . . . I was on the street slightly over two hours and I can say I've never seen such entertainment anywhere. . . . I know I'll never forget what I've seen, and there are millions like me.

Louis and Judy Funderburg celebrated their fifty-fifth wedding anniversary on New Year's Day, 2000, which Louis describes with a chuckle as "a good start" to a next century.

BEFORE WORLD WAR II, PARENTAL approval was widely regarded as necessary for a respectable marriage. Of course, some couples eloped in order to circumvent disapproving parents, but that usually led to a trail of gossip. The war changed these rules. Every day, all across America, young people who had known each other only a few months, weeks, or even days rushed off to get married, and in many instances, parents didn't even know about the relationship. But then there were quite different cases in which a parent—or grandparent—was actually the first to know that a wedding was about to happen, even before the bride and groom did.

*Hugh and Maudie Owens on their wedding day,*
*December 19, 1945, in San Francisco.*

# Hugh and Maudie
## OWENS

Maudie Matthews was attending Utah State University in 1942, away from her hometown, and living with her grandmother. A women's group on campus organized many social events to make soldiers in the area feel more at home, and one day Maudie was talked into attending one of these events. She found it terribly boring and vowed never to go to another. But when the quarter ended, most of the young women on campus headed home for the break, and with such a shortage of women left on campus for social functions, she was persuaded to do her duty and make one more appearance.

This time things were more lively, particularly after Hugh Owens, a marine who was attending radio material school at the college, struck up an engaging conversation with her. They had a wonderful time dancing, even though, as Maudie found out later, Hugh didn't really like to dance and had made a special effort because he was so taken with her. Despite restrictive rules for young women on campus regarding how to behave with young military men, when Hugh asked Maudie for her telephone number, she decided to give it to him.

Hugh called her the very next day and asked her to dinner that evening. She was pleased to hear from him, especially so quickly, and she suggested that they go to a nice restaurant in town called the Bluebird. They had such a good time that she started seeing Hugh regularly.

Maudie's grandmother, a tiny woman with a strong personality, was generally dismissive of young men who tried to court Maudie, but she liked Hugh immediately. He came to dinner on Sundays, and almost every week, Maudie's grandmother baked her special chocolate pie for him. "Grandmother also made beautiful quilts," Maudie remembers, "and one day I noticed that she was working on a new one." When Maudie asked her who the quilt was for, "she looked up at me and said, 'Why, you and Hugh, eventually.'" Maudie remembers thinking that her grandmother was getting a little ahead of things, but perhaps not all that much.

After Hugh finished radio material school, he was assigned to Treasure Island, off the coast of San Francisco, for another five months of training. While he was still in the U.S., Hugh wrote regularly, but when he shipped out to the South Pacific, his letters dwindled. She understood that: There was a war on, after all, and mail from the South Pacific took even longer to reach the States than mail from the European theater.

Back in Utah, Maudie grew restless and decided to join one of the services. She chose the navy—in large part, she now admits, because she thought the Waves had the prettiest uniforms. Maudie's mother wasn't exactly enthusiastic about the idea, but she finally agreed it would be all right as long as Maudie wasn't sent overseas; at that point in the war, Waves were not being sent for overseas postings.

Before making her final decision, Maudie also wrote Hugh a letter to ask him what he thought. Weeks went by without reply, so she decided to go ahead and sign up.

Like many other Waves, Maudie was sent east to New York's Hunter College for boot camp, then was assigned to San Francisco for training as a recruiter. After several months in San Francisco, she was assigned to a recruiting post in Salt Lake City, Utah. Ironically, she finally heard back from Hugh, who gave her the "go-ahead," and she was pleased to know he approved of the decision she'd long since made.

By this time, Hugh was assigned to the Twelfth Anti-Aircraft Battalion at Pearl Harbor. From there, his battalion was shipped out to Townsville, Australia, a major staging point for the war in the South Pacific. Subsequently, the battalion was stationed at Woodlark Island to protect the construction crew building an airstrip there. After that, they moved on to New Guinea, where a major front was opened against the Japanese in April 1944. Luckily for Hugh, he missed most of the difficult fighting in New Guinea because he had applied for officer training and was shipped back to the U.S.

Two openings for officer's positions in his battalion had come up, one as a warrant officer and the other as a second lieutenant. Both Hugh and a friend applied, and because the friend was too old to be commissioned as a second lieutenant, he ended up with the warrant officer's position and stayed with the battalion, while Hugh got the second lieutenant spot and was sent to Quantico, Virginia, for "ninety-day-wonder" officer's training.

After Hugh received his officer's commission, he was given three weeks' leave, and he went to visit his family in Topeka, Kansas. Maudie was delighted to receive a letter from him asking if she could come see him there, which meant that their relationship was becoming more serious. Maybe her grandmother had been right after all.

Because Maudie hadn't taken any leave yet, she had no trouble getting the time; but her trip to Topeka and back was a roundabout journey, to say the least. First she took the train from Salt Lake City to San Francisco to collect her leave papers. Then she headed back across the country to Topeka, where she stayed with Hugh's sister, who treated her wonderfully. On her return, she traveled all the way back to San Francisco before finally heading to Utah. Understandably, she was thoroughly sick of train travel by the time her leave was over.

But the trip was well worth the effort. Sure enough, during her stay, Hugh proposed, and Maudie immediately accepted. Hugh was being stationed in Hawaii right after his leave, and he busily set about buying Maudie an engagement ring, which he promised he'd send before he left.

When she returned to Utah, Maudie was reassigned to a new town, Ogden, where, as was typical for recruiters, she worked out of the main post office. Of course she shared her good news with her recruitment colleagues and the postal workers, and told them she was expecting her engagement ring in the mail. But then she waited day after day for the package from Hugh with no sign. To her chagrin, one of the male recruiters took to kidding her about whether or not the package would ever show up. Finally, after he apparently felt the joke had gone on long enough—maybe too long, Maudie thought—he handed her the package, which he had spotted when it arrived and had been hiding from her.

Back on Hawaii, Hugh had been assigned to administrative duties, but in mid-1945, he suddenly got the word that he was on draft to be sent to China. Luck prevailed for him once again, however, when his doctor recommended that he go in for a minor surgical procedure before heading overseas. For some reason that Hugh still can't comprehend, he was kept in the hospital for forty days after the procedure. By the time he was released, not only was his tour of duty up, but the war was over. Instead of heading to China, he was sent back to the mainland to be mustered out in Great Lakes, Michigan.

Hugh and Maudie were married on December 19, 1945, in San Francisco, where Maudie had been sent after her assignment in Ogden. Their most prized wedding gift was from Maudie's grandmother: the double-ring quilt she had started making early in Maudie and Hugh's relationship. They used the quilt for so many years that their two sons, Parker and David, were grown men by the time the quilt was in its final decline.

Hugh in his Marine Corps uniform, before he received his officer's commission.

Hugh, now a second lieutenant, in his new officer's uniform, with Maudie in her Waves uniform and his parents, Evelyn and Park, at their home in Topeka.

Hugh and Maudie on a cruise through the Panama Canal in March 1996.

ONE OF THE STRIKING FEATURES of the World War II experience is the role that chance played, both in the fates of those soldiers fortunate enough to survive the bullets and bombs, and in so many of the brief encounters that sparked lifelong romances. For the soldiers, they could never know when they might find themselves under fire; but on the other hand, they might be lucky enough to find themselves mysteriously selected for special attention by a young woman making the most of her opportunities for finding Mr. Right.

*Harold and Adelle Jensen on their wedding day,*
*November 6, 1943.*

# *Harold and Adelle*

## JENSEN

Harold Jensen joined the army in 1939 because, as he says, "the Depression was on and we couldn't get jobs. We were also too poor to go to school other than high school, and the military was advertising with posters saying 'We Want You,' so I joined." A year later, on January 9, 1940, he joined the army air corps and a month after that was assigned to Hickam Field at Pearl Harbor, as a mechanic and crew chief on a B-18 bomber. Hawaii was a great posting because of the beautiful weather, but Harold recalls that the trip to the islands, which now is a relatively easy flight, took him a full month, including passage through the Panama Canal. Harold had always dreamed of being a pilot, and after a year and a half, in July 1941, he applied and was accepted for pilot training. He was still awaiting transportation back to the States for training when, on December 7, at 7:53 in the morning of yet another gorgeous Hawaiian day, the first wave of squadron after squadron of Japanese bombers—353 in all—swooped down on Pearl Harbor, taking the forces there and at the nearby airfields by surprise. Harold recalls that "they just blew the devil out of us."

Although the greatest loss of life in the attack took place in the harbor itself, especially on the battleships *Arizona* and *Oklahoma,* Hickam Field was also hard hit. One bomb landed directly on the mess hall at the field, where thirty-five pilots were eating breakfast, and killed them all. The planes at the field, parked wingtip to wingtip, were sitting ducks for the Japanese bombers, and eighteen were destroyed before they could get off the ground.

Harold was awakened by the attack when a bomb hit the building next to his barracks. He remembers thinking that "it was the navy goofing off," running fire drills. But when a bomb crashed through the roof of his barracks just minutes later, he realized the attack was for real. As the crew chief of his bomber, his primary responsibility was for the safety of the plane, and he rushed to the hangar to find that a bomb had exploded right next to his plane. "You know, it was full of holes," he recalls, "but we took it out and patched it up later on." He also remembers that the Japanese planes were trying to shoot down an American flag atop a flagpole, swooping down low over the barracks in repeated attempts. "They were strafing, too," he recounts, "and there were lots of guys laying around. Most of them dead." Harold started helping move men from the hangar to the medical facility on the base, and while he was assisting one man, a close friend of his, a bomb hit only about forty feet away, throwing Harold against the wall of the hangar. Shrapnel from the bomb tore into his arm, but Harold kept moving men. Many men lost most of their hearing temporarily from of the incredibly loud noise of the bombs.

Because Harold was one of the few soldiers on base who had access to a truck, he was sent to a nearby army post, Fort Kamehameha, to bring back stretchers. On his way back, he saw a Japanese plane fixing its sights on him, and he rushed out of his truck. "He was zeroing in on me, I'll guarantee you, because anything that moved, they'd strafe." Harold was shot in the shin. Not only was he worried that he would no longer be able to go to flight school, he was even more anxious about the (unfounded) rumors that the Japanese coated their bullets with poison. He was laid up in the hospital for several weeks after the attack.

Despite his worries, he was not prohibited from flight school, though he had to wait many more months before he could start. Finally, in July he left for the States for his training, after which he was assigned as a flight instructor in cargo gliders at an airbase in Lubbock, Texas. A few weeks after he arrived, an epidemic of trench mouth hit the flight line. A number of soldiers, including Harold, went to the base dental clinic for treatment. When Harold showed up for his first treatment, he was quite taken with the receptionist, a very pretty blonde. He'd been told there were a lot of pretty young women in Texas, and this receptionist "certainly fit the bill." But he also noticed that she was wearing an engagement ring, so he kept his interest to himself.

A few days after his first treatment, Harold had to report back to the dental clinic for additional care. The same receptionist greeted him warmly. He made note, with surprise, that she was no longer wearing the engagement ring, and wondered what the story was. After a few more days, he received notice of yet another appointment, and this time he managed to find out that the receptionist's name was Adelle Taylor.

When he had been called back several more times for clinic appointments, Harold began to wonder just what was going on. As far as he could tell, his trench mouth was fully cured. But he didn't much mind, because every time he went to the clinic, he had the chance to chat with the beautiful Adelle Taylor, and he was finally emboldened to ask her for a date. She quickly accepted. They got along wonderfully, and before long, Adelle confessed that she had been attracted to him from the start and had set him up. Turns out that the dental hygienist at the clinic was a good friend of hers and had agreed to keep Harold coming back for treatments that weren't really necessary. Adelle had also taken the precaution of checking Harold's medical file to see if he was married; in the past, she explained, a couple of soldiers had lied to her about their marital status.

Harold and Adelle dated very happily for several months, but then he got word that a search-and-rescue squadron was being formed in Denver, and he felt the call to volunteer. He thought this work was truly important and didn't want to pass up such an opportunity. His transfer might have spelled the end of their time together, but just before he left, Harold asked Adelle if she would wait for him—for who knew how long—until they could be married. She accepted, and when he gave her an engagement ring, she promised to keep this one on.

Their wait, as things turned out, wasn't long at all. Immediately upon arriving in Denver, Harold was informed that the new squadron had been canceled, and he was happily reassigned to Lubbock. He and Adelle were married there in November 1943. "We've been on our honeymoon ever since," Harold now quips. While many servicemen during World War II met their wives while recuperating in hospital wards, Harold figures there

# *Harold and Adelle* JENSEN

*Harold while in
pilot school in 1942.*

*Harold living it up on Waikiki Beach in
Honolulu in 1941.*

*Harold and Adelle as proud parents
in Lubbock, Texas, in 1944.*

The envelope carrying a letter from Adelle to Harold while he was serving combat duty in the Korean War, which apparently went through quite a few hands and took two months to reach him.

Harold and Adelle on their fifty-sixth wedding anniversary.

aren't many who can say there were brought together by a suspiciously lingering case of trench mouth.

After the war, he stayed in the service and retired as a career officer in the United States Air Force after twenty-two years of active duty, a good part of that overseas. He completed one combat tour during the Korean War, as well as two other overseas tours, including one in Taiwan, for which Adelle and their two sons joined him. After retiring from the air force, Harold worked at the White Sands Missile Range as a civil service range controller engineer for an additional seventeen years, retiring for good in 1978. Married for fifty-seven years, the couple still lives in New Mexico.

W OMEN CERTAINLY WEREN'T
*the only ones who knew how to make*
*the most out of a chance encounter.*
*So many men and women met during the war purely*
*by accident, spent a pleasant enough hour or so together,*
*and then, despite the attraction they might feel, never*
*saw each other again. But for some lucky couples, the*
*hand of fate brought them together again. The question*
*whether such a second meeting was really the work of*
*fate, or was cleverly orchestrated, was an issue they*
*were happy to leave a mystery.*

*Marjorie and Jack Vaira shortly after they became engaged, while vacationing at the seafront resort town of Torquay in April 1944.*

# Jack and Marjorie
## VAIRA

Marjorie Vaira was born in Plymouth, England, on the coast of Devon, in May 1924. She grew up in this most southerly of England's important channel ports, from which the Pilgrims sailed to America in 1620.

The Battle of Britain raged from July to October 1940, but Plymouth escaped the worst of the damage. In the spring of 1941, though, Hitler ordered two direct bombing attacks on Plymouth, each of which lasting for three days. These attacks were partly in retaliation for a recent rash of deadly bombings of German U-boats; three of the submarines sunk by the Brits had been captained by personal favorites of Hitler. During the second assault, Marjorie's home was destroyed, forcing the seventeen-year-old and her mother to take shelter with relatives for several months. In September, Marjorie's mother managed to buy a house in South Brent, an inland village of about two thousand people.

Then eighteen, Marjorie found a job with the British War Department Land Agency, which had also moved inland from the virtually destroyed Plymouth. The agency's function was to requisition land to house the American and British troops who were gradually being assembled for the coming invasion of Europe. Marjorie was accustomed to a rather exciting city life and quickly realized she would have to make a special effort to entertain herself in this inland village. So she was happy enough to volunteer some evenings at the canteen established by the British counterpart of America's USO.

On the night of January 11, 1944, Marjorie was walking the half mile from her home to the canteen in a heavy downpour when she saw two murky "shapes" in the night. Slightly worried, Marjorie called out a good evening. Two voices, which seemed friendly enough, replied.

Shortly after Marjorie got to the canteen, she saw two American officers enter, and soon recognized their voices as those of the shapes in the darkness. The officers, whose unit had arrived only that morning, asked what entertainment was available in South Brent. Then the officer who did most of the talking offered Marjorie a challenge. "I hear you English can't make coffee," he said. Marjorie couldn't let his comment pass and coyly replied, "You can come home with me, and my mother and I will make you some." Both of the officers accepted and walked her home. When they left, after coffee and pleasantries, it occurred to Marjorie that she might never see either of them again.

Fate would not allow that. The next morning, Marjorie found a leather glove on the outside doormat. At work, she managed to get the telephone number of the camp where the officers were stationed. She told the soldier who answered the phone about the found glove, but she couldn't remember the name of the lieutenant who had left it. She knew simply that his last name began with a "V." That's all she needed to know. The soldier knew it had to be Lieutenant Vaira—the only man in the place with a last name starting with "V." Marjorie asked the soldier to tell Lieutenant Vaira that he could collect his glove at her house if he wanted it back. That evening, Jack Vaira returned to her house to claim his glove and laid claim to her heart as well.

Jack's battalion, the 149th Engineer Combat, was stationed at South Brent for just ten days, after which they were transferred to Paignton, about twenty-five miles away. Jack and Marjorie saw each other only on weekends and had to travel by train to do so. Marjorie remembers that the last train left Paignton at nine P.M. "Not very romantic," she comments dryly.

Early in April, after just four months of dating, Jack asked Marjorie's father for permission to marry her. Her father agreed, and Jack and Marjorie considered themselves engaged, even though Jack had not yet been able to secure a ring. Later in April 1944, all troops were sequestered in preparation for D-Day. Marjorie did not see Jack again for nearly a year.

Jack was in the first wave of troops to land on Omaha Beach, where the greatest number of casualties occurred. The troops had great difficulty getting tanks and artillery onshore; once they were ashore, the best defending German division lay in wait for them, aided considerably by the surrounding cliffs and steep dunes. Marjorie would not know how terrible D-Day had been until much later, but luckily, Jack survived it.

Once Omaha Beach was secured, the American forces, somewhat miraculously, received a mail delivery. Jack had been waiting for a small package, which he finally got. He met with the captain of a ship that carried supplies to Omaha Beach from Plymouth, and asked him if he could take the package back to England and see that it was delivered.

In early August, Marjorie arrived home for lunch to find two American sailors waiting for her. Their captain had dispatched them from Plymouth during a layover to deliver Jack's package: In it were Marjorie's engagement and wedding rings.

In a letter, Jack told Marjorie that he had been promised the first leave after the war ended. His colonel kept his word, and Jack finally returned to England on Saturday, May 12, 1945. He and Marjorie wanted to be married at once, but first they had to get a license. Also, Marjorie had agreed to take the female lead in a local drama-society production of *Poison Pen*. How could she have known the war would end when it did? Her acting group was too small to have understudies, so Marjorie had to go on.

On May 17, the show's last night, Marjorie and Jack were married at three-forty-five P.M. that afternoon (the latest hour a wedding could be performed). Jack sat in the audience for Marjorie's final performance. "I believe he was as much 'on show' as I was," Marjorie says with a laugh, since everyone in town knew about the wedding. After wildly applauding his brand-new wife at the last curtain, Jack set off with Marjorie on their honeymoon.

Jack served for a year in the army of occupation in Germany, where Marjorie joined him. In 1947 they returned to America together on the troop ship *Willard A. Holbrook*.

They lived with great happiness until Jack's death in 1988. But Marjorie never did figure out the answer to one important question: She never found out whether Jack left that glove on her doorstep on purpose.

Jack and fellow officers on the seafront after their arrival at Paignton. Left to right: Captain Shumaker; Lieutenant Brown; Jack; and Lieutenant Romanek, the "coffee taster."

Jack with a "four-footed French friend" on Omaha Beach, after the army had secured it.

Jack and Marjorie just after their wedding ceremony in front of the South Brent Methodist Church, on May 17, 1945.

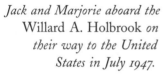

*Jack and Marjorie aboard the*
Willard A. Holbrook *on
their way to the United
States in July 1947.*

*Jack and Marjorie, at
left, during a reunion
of the 149th Engineer
Combat Brigade in
Kansas City with Beryl
Newell and his wife,
Laura, the only other
bride from South Brent
of a 149ther.*

ROMANCE BROKE AS MANY HEARTS *as it sent soaring during World War II. Men fighting battles around the world saw so many friends wounded or killed that they became fatalistic about their own physical well-being. They came to see the fighting itself as a kind of lottery. You did your best and you either ended up lucky or you didn't. But while they may have become inured to the possibility of physical danger, many could not so easily escape the profound dread of a Dear John letter arriving from a sweetheart or a wife back home, announcing that a new love had entered their lives. And of course, the women back home often worried their man might find someone else to love in a busy port or bombed-out city halfway around the globe. But more often, it came to pass that romance, even that of fairy-tale proportions, was undone not by the fickleness of love but by one unlucky shell on the battlefield.*

*Eddie Swauger and Catherine Roberts leaving the Church
of St. Mary the Virgin on the Tidworth House grounds
after their wedding ceremony on February 19, 1943.*

# Catherine M.

# ROBERTS-SWAUGER

When Catherine Roberts first tried to join the women's auxiliary air force of England's Royal Air Force in the summer of 1941, her recruiting officer, a gray-haired flight sergeant with a pencil mustache, threw up his hands in bewilderment. Her papers said she was an American, and Americans were not allowed to join the WAAF. The young woman in the smart gray suit protested vehemently. Although she had been born in America to an American couple, she had been adopted by a Welsh couple and raised in Wales, and she thought of herself as Welsh. Besides, she pointed out, everyone knew there were lots of Americans in the RAF—which was true. Many young Americans who had wanted to join the war against Hitler before the United States officially entered had traveled to Canada in hopes of circumventing the rules. The recruiter explained to Catherine that those Americans were now considered Canadians, so Catherine's protests went unheeded.

Catherine had been born in Boston, Massachusetts, on March 4, 1920, to a German-American paperhanger named Barnard Abbot and his bride, Amanda, a Penobscot Indian. Six months later, the couple gave her up for adoption to Griffith and Dora Roberts. Griffith born in Wales, had run away to sea at thirteen, seen much of the world, joined the U.S. Navy in 1890, and fought in the Spanish-American War. He returned to Wales to see his family and stole the beautiful Dora from all the local Lotharios. He returned to America in 1910 with Dora as his bride. He served in the

U.S. Navy during World War I, then retired from the navy after twenty-eight years' service.

Dora had five miscarriages, and Catherine's adoption in 1920 brought the couple great happiness at last. In 1926, Griffith felt the pull of home once more, and he and Dora returned for good to the coastal town of Penryhyndeudraeth, Wales, with their adopted American daughter.

As a grown woman, Catherine became determined to play a real part in the war, even if her complicated origins made things difficult. She harassed both the British Air Ministry and the American embassy until she was finally told to write to General Dwight D. Eisenhower, who was visiting England in an advisory capacity. Her letter actually generated a response, and at last she gained permission to apply for enrollment in the WAAF. She reported to the RAF at Bridgnorth, Gloucestershire, on December 12, 1941—five days after Pearl Harbor brought the United States into the war.

Catherine found the next eight months quite intense. She had to withstand the rigors of training, including a daunting solo introduction to the use of a gas mask in a claustrophobic chamber. And she had adventures that she would remember for a lifetime. Late one drizzly afternoon, she stepped into a warm upscale pub. An American officer noticed the U.S.A. insignia on her British uniform and asked about it. She was surprised that he did not introduce himself—she'd noticed that Americans usually did the moment you met them. He did look awfully familiar, though she couldn't think quite why. When another American officer strolled up to join them, the answer hit her with quite a jolt: The strolling army air force colonel was unmistakably the lanky Jimmy Stewart, who'd starred in so many of her favorite movies; and the man with the big grin she had been talking to, she suddenly realized, was none other than Clark Gable.

Amid all the excitement of training and meeting soldiers from all over the world, Catherine was having some romantic difficulties. Two old flames, Jamie and William, had a hold on her heart, and both were in love with her. Yet her feelings toward them seemed to depend on which one she happened to be with at a particular moment, or whose letter she held in her hand.

In August 1942 she had an experience that made the decision for her—and changed her life forever. One morning, she saw an invitation to a dance posted on the notice board: "All ranks of the WAAF at RAF Old Sarum are invited to a dance to be held at Tidworth House, the ancestral home of the Duchess of Marlborough, this coming Saturday evening. Transport there and back will be provided by the U.S. Army. All who wish to avail themselves of this invitation are to assemble at the Guardroom at 1900 hours." Catherine decided to go. Tidworth House, she knew, had been lent to the American Red Cross as its headquarters, with Mrs. Teddy Roosevelt (the president's cousin by marriage) running things. She thought it would be grand to at least get a look at the famous mansion.

The band that night played "Don't Fence Me In" and "Little Brown Jug" and "Chattanooga Choo-Choo" for jiving to, and "I'll Remember You," "Stardust," and "As Time Goes By" for partners to draw a little closer. During a lull, as she was chatting with two friends, "a tall, blond Nordic type approached." He addressed her in a manner that she was certain came straight from the *U.S. Soldier's Guidebook to Britain:* "May I have the pleasure of the next dance, please?"

She nodded, the band struck up again, and she stepped forward to join him.

The soldier introduced himself as Eddie Swauger from Beaver, Pennsylvania. "I see that you have the U.S.A. badge on the shoulder of your British uniform," he said to Catherine. "How come?"

Lots of American men had asked that question of Catherine, even Clark Gable. But, Catherine clearly recalls, as the words fell from Eddie's lips, something came over her, taking her completely by surprise. For the first time in her life, she found herself head over heels in love at first sight. Thoughts of William and Jamie, about whom she'd been worrying and moping for days, suddenly vanished.

When the band stopped, Catherine remembers, "Eddie winked mischievously and said, 'Let's stay on the floor. I just can't risk anyone else taking you away now.'" For the rest of the evening, Eddie and Catherine danced rapturously and talked endlessly. Eddie told her about his small hometown, his trips into Pittsburgh with pals, and his weekend sailing excursions to Danesville on Lake Erie. He told her of being the youngest of three children, of his mother's death when he was only three years old, and of his father's remarriage to a woman with two sons. He told her how he dreamed of becoming a veterinary surgeon specializing in horses in the Blue Grass country of Kentucky. In turn, Catherine told him the story of her own unique past. When the evening ended, they eagerly agreed to meet again.

They saw each other again in Salisbury. Eddie had the evening all planned. "Come on," he urged her, "we're just in time to see one of the funniest films for years. It's Jack Benny and Kay Francis in *Charlie's Aunt.* We can go to the first show at the new picture house and still have time for something to eat and a drink afterwards." Catherine was utterly delighted. She told him how her family used to gather around the wireless to listen to the *Jack Benny Show* each week, and how hard she had laughed at the cinema in Barmouth, Wales, when she saw him in *Buck Benny Rides Again.* Suddenly she remembered that Jamie had been right at her side laughing along with her that day; but she pushed that thought out of her mind.

Catherine and Eddie saw each other frequently at Tidworth House dances, which were held five nights a week, with different combinations of servicemen and -women invited each time. They always got along wonderfully, until one day Eddie did something that shocked and very much disappointed Catherine. Catherine had been looking forward to the annual Charity Ball at the Salisbury Guild Hall for weeks. She had gone out of her way to make special arrangements to be off duty the evening of the ball. She had even borrowed a beautiful evening gown for the occasion. But Eddie clean forgot the date. Oblivious to Catherine's excitement and planning, he had agreed to attend the town's Welfare Committee meeting that night. When Catherine found out, she reacted with a "short but sharp explosion." Remaining calm, Eddie promised to work something out. "Don't worry, Cinderella must go to the ball," he said, and pulled her close to kiss her nose.

After pulling a few strings, Eddie found a friend to take his place at the meeting. He and Catherine attended the ball together, and both found it a thrilling occasion that more than justified its reputation as the "social event of the year."

As they strolled toward the RAF trucks waiting to transport people home, Catherine inquired about his interest in the welfare meeting, and asked whether he'd always been involved with other people's problems. Eddie, a bit sheepishly, said he guessed he had. He'd started his involvement in a choir at school that had raised money for elderly people's homes. He told her that while his family had been far from rich, his parents had always taken care of him. But he knew that thousands of kids had to manage on next to nothing. He didn't think of himself as a do-gooder and said he was merely trying to assuage his own guilt at the unfairness of things.

Hearing his quiet, eloquent words, Catherine stopped walking and kissed him, "lovingly at first, and then passionately," she remembers. She could hardly speak as they walked on. She felt like crying, she was so in love with this man from Beaver, Pennsylvania.

Eddie's involvement with the Welfare Committee wasn't his only act of service. Although only a private, Eddie had been enormously helpful to Mrs. Teddy Roosevelt. Whenever a special problem developed at Tidworth House, she always suggested calling on Eddie to fix it.

Catherine came to marvel at Eddie's remarkable ability to take charge and get things done, even those that seemed impossible. One day early in their relationship, she missed the bus back to her billet and had to accept a ride from an officer on a motorcycle. There was no real place to put her feet, so she just let them dangle. Just before they reached her billet, she let out a shriek, and the officer pulled the motorcycle to an abrupt halt. Catherine instantly tumbled off onto the ground in terror. Her shoe had caught fire—she'd been holding it over the searing exhaust pipe.

When she told Eddie what had happened, he took her shoes back to base with him and returned them with new soles—hardly an easy task in wartime Britain, where all materials were strictly rationed. So she wasn't all that surprised that Mrs. Roosevelt thought Eddie a treasure, too, even though she did tease him about it.

One day, Eddie teased her back. "You'll never guess what Mrs. Roosevelt said to me this morning," he said.

"That you were the handsomest GI in Britain?" Catherine suggested.

"No," said Eddie, and paused. "I don't think I should tell you."

"Don't be a tease." As Catherine looks back at their conversation, she remembers having a powerful sense at that moment that she was about to hear something related to her dearest wish in the world.

Eddie laughed and said, "Well, she said that if we ever thought about getting engaged to be married, we just had to let her know and she would give us a party to mark the occasion of the first American in the WAAF to marry a GI."

Before Catherine could say a word, Eddie jumped up and ran off, calling over his shoulder, "And now you can report me to your CC for careless talk."

Soon enough, the promised engagement party took place. Catherine was absolutely thrilled by the event. But when Mrs. Roosevelt "and her equally imperious friend, the Duchess of Marlborough," to whom Tidworth House belonged, began eagerly planning a wedding reception there, Catherine found herself a bit taken aback. Secretly, she had always hoped for a quiet wedding in Wales.

It soon became clear to her that the zealous enthusiasm of Mrs. Roosevelt and the Duchess stemmed not merely from their good wishes for the couple, but also from their desire to play off of the avid interest *Life* magazine had shown in the engagement party. A wedding reception would cap Catherine and Eddie's fairy-tale story—surely bolstering Anglo-American relations.

February 19, 1943, the wedding day, was cloudless and bright, quite unusual in England at that time of year. Catherine's parents had arrived in Salisbury earlier in the week, enjoying frequent and relaxing excursions into the countryside after weeks of scurrying around to collect clothing coupons from friends and relatives who could spare a few for Catherine to have a lovely traditional wedding gown. Flowers, thanks to careful planning by Eddie and Mrs. Roosevelt, were plentiful and beautiful. The wedding party, clothed in their fine attire, gathered excitedly to wait in the foyer of the hotel. Catherine's matron of honor wore a lovely pink gown, and the three bridesmaids turned out in their "best blue" uniforms with burnished brass buttons glistening brightly. Catherine's father waited with them, too, while her mother, the groom, and best man went ahead to the ancient Gothic Episcopalian Church of St. Mary the Virgin on the Tidworth House grounds.

After several minutes, Catherine made a stunning appearance at the top of the hotel stairs. "Stop right there!" a voice called out. Photographers from *Life* and the Associated Press rushed forward. Flashbulbs popped everywhere. Mrs. Roosevelt and the Duchess of Marlborough certainly would succeed in getting their full measure of symbolism and publicity out of the event.

But Catherine's father, knew from his own navy experience that the officers at the church should not be kept waiting. This ceremony needed to begin on time. He stepped forward to take charge, keeping overzealous photographers at bay so the wedding party could push past the crowd.

Eddie's commanding officer, Colonel McNeary, had given the whole of his unit the afternoon off to attend the ceremony. Mrs. Roosevelt greeted hundreds of guests as they arrived at the church in military limousines, staff cars, jeeps, trucks, even a half-track or two. The three hundred guests were seated, rows of U.S. Army khaki on the left, Royal Air Force blue on the right.

An organ prelude began the ceremony, followed by the first chords of Handel's "Arrival of the Queen of Sheba." As the majestic chords resonated through the church, Catherine began the walk down the aisle on the arm of her father. As Eddie and Catherine performed their vows and the ceremony continued, Private Marty McKenna, importing an American tradition, raised his dulcet tenor voice in renditions of "O Promise Me" and "I Love You Truly."

After the very successful ceremony, the Duchess of Marlborough and Mrs. Teddy Roosevelt led the way out of the church and across the oak-lined driveway back to Tidworth House. As the guests arrived, they gasped when they saw the lavish spread: platefuls of sliced honey-baked ham, salmon, roast pork, Cornish pasties, and sausage rolls of many kinds. Bowls of pineapple chunks, apricots, and peach slices stood between huge dishes of cream-topped trifle. There were American doughnuts, too. Mrs. Roosevelt flew much of the food in from the United States. "I didn't think there was that much food left in the world," one of Catherine's bridesmaids whispered.

On a table to one side stood the centerpiece of the reception: a three-tiered wedding cake that Eddie's unit ordered from the States. Press photographers scrambled everywhere to record the event. Even when

Catherine and Eddie left the reception and went to the Salisbury railway station for their trip to the Strand Hotel in London, where they would spend their brief honeymoon, the photographers followed. The American novelist and journalist Faith Baldwin awaited the couple at the station, where she interviewed them and took photographs for her own magazine. She informed them that President Roosevelt had specially requested a set of her photos.

Catherine and Eddie spent a luxurious but all too short honeymoon at the Strand Hotel. Then, right away, they each had to return to the demands of wartime duties. Eddie's division was about to begin a series of rigorous training exercises for amphibious assault landings. Meetings between the newlyweds became increasingly rare. As they parted at the end of one of their fleeting reunions, Eddie whispered in her ear, "Maybe when I come back from this exercise, I'll be a prospective father!"

Indeed, when Catherine went home on leave to visit her parents at the end of April, she felt queasy on two successive mornings. She said nothing to her parents but reported to the infirmary as soon as she got back to RAF Old Sarum. The doctor confirmed her suspicion: She was pregnant. Her days with the women's auxiliary air force would soon be over. On May 17, 1943, she was given an allowance of twelve pounds and ten shillings for civilian clothing and dismissed from the ranks of leading aircraftwomen.

Catherine returned home to her parents in Wales, where Eddie was able to see her only once, during a seven-day leave in October. On November 24, Catherine gave birth to a baby daughter whom they named Catherine and called Babsie for short. Eddie was thankfully given an unexpected "compassionate" leave to visit his wife and child. When he saw Babsie's blue eyes and curly golden hair, he said to Catherine, "Now I've got everything I ever wanted."

But the war still raged on. While Catherine tried to cope alone with her new baby and the rationing that stood in such stark contrast to the lavishness of their wedding feast, Eddie continued training for the invasion of Europe that everyone knew would come eventually.

On April 26, 1944, Eddie had the misfortune to be part of the disastrous large-scale exercise at Slapton Sands, between Dartmouth and Plymouth on the channel coast. Everything that could go wrong did. After all the mishaps, in a dramatic climax, German torpedo boats attacked the soldiers, killing more than seven hundred. Ten officers missing after the attack possessed confidential information regarding the United States' plans for D-Day. Had they been captured, all the plans would have had to be changed, for fear the captured might succumb to German torture tactics and spill crucial details. But, one by one, their dead bodies were recovered—a horrific sort of mixed blessing. Miraculously, Eddie came through this debacle unscathed. But like all the other soldiers who had taken part, he had gained a new and vivid sense of what they would face in a real invasion. Due to military censorship, he could communicate none of this to Catherine, so she remained unaware of the magnitude of danger her husband regularly faced.

Eddie would survive the D-Day invasion. He would survive the Battle of Hurtgen Forest in the autumn, in which thirty thousand Americans were killed or wounded. But his luck ran out, all too soon, during the infamous Battle of the Bulge.

A horrific counteroffensive by the Germans that began on December 16, 1944, the Battle of the Bulge left eighty thousand Americans and twenty-five hundred British soldiers dead, wounded, or in German captivity. Eddie was shot in the head, which left shrapnel lodged in his skull. Catherine received word in Wales that he was being sent to a hospital in the United States.

Catherine had to wait an entire year for Eddie's release from the hospital, whereupon she could finally join him in America. Finally, Eddie healed well enough to leave hospital grounds, and in April 1946, Catherine boarded a GI-bride transport ship, the *Bridgeport,* with Babsie, now two and a half years old.

After the long voyage across the Atlantic, Catherine finally saw the love of her life waiting for her on the dock in New York. But when she got to him, she realized that the man on that dock was no longer the Eddie she had known. "He was a stranger in civilian clothes," Catherine wrote in her journal. "The tall, blond, Nordic-looking man who courted me at Tidworth and Salisbury had gone. Now there was a man who seemed to have shrunk. He stooped and had a patch of sparse hair covering an ugly red cicatrix of a wound rising from his temple." Eddie still had shrapnel in his brain.

He took Catherine and their daughter to his hometown in Pennsylvania, but from the start, he and Catherine faced problems. Although his wounds appeared to have healed, the war had scarred Eddie's mind. In those days, post-traumatic stress disorder was not the common phrase it is today. Little was understood about the ravaging effect war could have on the psyche. Eddie never got the psychological help he needed to recover his lost self.

Just as Catherine was learning to cope with the changes in her relationship with Eddie, fate dealt her another blow. Her parents had preceded her to the United States by two months, moving back to Medford, Massachusetts, where Catherine had lived as a child. Suddenly, after an illness of just a few months, Catherine's father died. Another bulwark was gone from her life.

One afternoon Catherine returned home after taking Babsie for a walk to find Eddie packing. He had decided to rejoin the army. In the spring of 1947, they divorced, and Catherine moved east to be near her mother.

Now on her own with Babs, she enrolled at aviation training school. After graduation, she took a job with Trans Canada Airlines, which led to positions at Pan American, British Overseas Airways, and American Airlines. A hardworking employee, she worked her way up the corporate ladder from ground hostess to reservations agent to air freight administration.

Catherine, who had always loved to play the piano, also continued her studies at the Boston Conservatory of Music and gave a number of concerts. But mostly, she concentrated on raising her beautiful daughter, a living reminder of the joy she once had with Eddie. She never married again.

After thirty years with American Airlines, Catherine retired in 1980. A feisty soul, she couldn't endure sitting around the house, so she took a part-time job with a new branch of the USO welfare and entertainment organization that opened at Boston's Logan Airport. In 1984 she became full-time director of the Logan Airport center, and today, at eighty years old, she still works there as an assistant to the subsequent director.

Eddie Swauger, whom Catherine had loved so much, died in 1952. A fragment of the shrapnel in his brain moved suddenly, and in a few days he was gone. Looking back, Catherine has no regrets about marrying Eddie. She loved him deeply and still cherishes a thousand memories. Their daughter, who never knew the Eddie her mother had fallen in love with, blossomed into an exceptional woman.

Catherine fully accepts the life she has led. World War II blessed her with a great love, but then, as it did for so many others, it took that love away.

_Catherine Roberts in her WAAF uniform in 1941._

News photograph of the wedding reception at Tidworth House, with the standard Red Cross refreshments—doughnuts—on the table. From left: Mrs. Teddy Roosevelt; Catherine's father, Griffith Roberts; Catherine and Eddie; Catherine's mother, Dora Roberts.

Catherine Roberts-Swauger in 1999, then director of the Logan Airport USO in Boston, Massachusetts, with photo of USO hero Bob Hope.

WHILE MRS. TEDDY ROOSEVELT and a duchess lavishly celebrated the marriage of one lucky English bride to an American officer, many other romances between English girls and American GIs bloomed with less fanfare in the pubs and tight little houses in working-class districts. America had made its name as the land of opportunity, where anyone could dream of becoming president. The working-class girls involved with Americans heard a great deal about the modern wonders so common in the United States. Yet on occasion, an English girl who crossed the ocean after the war with her new American husband could find herself in for quite a shock.

*Floyd and Betty Bachman in Kansas City,*
*Missouri, in 1947.*

# *Betty Law*

## BACHMAN

Betty Law grew up in Burton-on-Trent, Staffordshire, England. On September 1, 1939, when she was nearly thirteen, fifty-three German divisions invaded Poland, leading the British and French to declare war on Germany on September 3. By June 4, 1940, the British retreat from Dunkirk was over, and Paris fell to Hitler's forces on June 14. Less than a month later, on July 10, the Battle of Britain began, and German bombs rained down on England.

Betty's mother and stepfather both worked in a munitions factory, and Betty took a job at fourteen. "We were needed," she later recalled, because so many men had gone away to war.

She has never forgotten the first bomb that affected her personally. Betty lived with her widowed grandmother at the time, and they were sitting in the living room when Betty heard a whistling bomb fly overhead. "I screamed and dropped my hot chocolate on the rug. Granny sat calmly drinking her nightly hot toddy and got angry with me for spilling my chocolate. 'It's miles away,' she said." In fact, the bomb dropped only about fifteen minutes away, blowing out her uncle Fred's windows and chimney stack and demolishing the houses across the street from him. After work, Betty ran to join everyone else in the neighborhood looking at the disaster scene. "I was standing on a mattress that had been blown from a bed. Under it they [later] found the [body of the] woman who had lived in that house."

A few months later, Betty's grandmother died. Betty returned to live with her mother, stepfather, three younger sisters, and two younger brothers. After one night spent in a cold concrete shelter, with all of them huddled together for hours, awaiting the all-clear, her mother—Betty called her Mam—declared, "No more. If we're going to die, we will do it in our own beds." And that was the last time the family ever went to a group shelter. As the war continued, people built smaller shelters on every street, but nobody ever used the one put up in Betty's family's backyard. In fact, her mother bought some chickens and used the shelter as a henhouse. They ate the chickens for Christmas and New Year's dinner.

Betty had been working for some time at Pirelli, a company that manufactured tires for military vehicles, until she began feeling ill. It turned out that she was allergic to rubber, so she took a new job with the Cooperative Society, delivering bread and cakes from a horse-drawn wagon. "On my job I had two routes, one Tuesday, Thursday, and Saturday, and the other Monday, Wednesday, and Friday. Each route had two hundred customers. I enjoyed it after I got used to working in all weather."

In addition to holding a job, all fifteen-year-olds were encouraged to join an auxiliary service of some kind. "I had to be different and joined the fire service. I tried to get in as a dispatcher, with a motorbike, but I was too young to do that, so I became a telephonist. We went on duty every other night from nine P.M. to eight A.M. We wore a uniform and carried a gas mask and a steel helmet. We were trained to identify different gases by smell. On duty we stayed in an air-raid shelter with two bunk beds and four phones. Two of us were on duty each night. My mate was named Joan. We took turns sleeping. Our job was to be prepared if an incendiary bomb dropped somewhere. When we got the call, we would find out what size fire engine and other equipment should go out. After I got off duty at eight A.M., I would go home, change, and go to work."

Betty does remember having some fun in the fire service. "Even though food was rationed, one of the firemen was a butcher, and he would bring liver. Someone else had an allotment plot for growing vegetables, and he'd bring potatoes and onions. There was usually someone to get hold of some black-market lard. So I would cook liver, onions, and chips while Joan took care of the phones. It really wasn't allowed, so Joan was supposed to buzz me if an officer came in. One day she couldn't buzz, so they caught me with my hands in the liver, all bloody. All I could do was brazen it out. I just invited them to eat with us. They didn't, but I got away with it."

When Betty turned eighteen in 1944, she was allowed to go with her mother to pubs, which were like working-class clubs in those days, for a drink on the nights she wasn't doing her fire service duty. Betty enjoyed those evenings, as they gave her a chance to really talk to her mother. "We were like sisters. I would tell her everything. As I grew up, she was the only one I could talk to. She always worked; we never had her at home during the day. I never got to be a kid, as I was the eldest and always had to help get dinner and take care of the other kids."

Yanks often hung around the pub. The Americans had been stationed in England from the time Betty was fifteen, so they were a familiar sight. "The Yanks used to think we were sisters. I didn't like that, but Mam did, as she felt younger. As I got older, though, I began to think it was funny and got to like it myself. Who would want people to know you were out with your mother?"

One night at the pub, an American named Larry Turner, whom Betty had talked to many times, as he was quite homesick, brought in a Yank sergeant and introduced him to Betty. His name was Floyd Bachman. Floyd asked if he could walk Betty home. "I said, 'Yes, if you can behave yourself.' Anyway, he took me home and didn't behave, and I slapped his face. I figured sure, just like all men, out for one thing, so when I saw him again, I wouldn't speak to him. Then one day Larry said, 'Come on, you kids' put Floyd's hand in mine, and said, 'Go.' Floyd took me home again." Floyd apologized for his earlier behavior, then asked Betty, "'Will you marry me?' I said, 'Don't be daft! I'm not marrying a Yank!' I went in the house and told my mother some bloody fool Yank asked me to marry him."

Nevertheless, Betty continued to go out with Floyd, who always acted as a gentleman after that first night. "At one point we had a major falling-out. For the next few weeks, it went like this: I would get home from work, and Larry would be there. He would say, 'Hi, kiddo, how are you?' I would say, 'fine.' He would say, 'That's great, but I know someone who isn't.' I would say, 'Too bad.' This went on night after night. I would have a date or go out with my mother for a drink, and in would walk some Yank, spot me, and go back out. Next Floyd would come in. If I had a date and he left for the bathroom, Floyd would sit in [his] spot. So I would leave. The same thing happened everywhere I went.

"Finally, one night when I was having a drink with Mam, I told Floyd he could walk me home if we all went together. We left, and when we got outside, Mam went one way and pushed us the other way. So we walked home, never spoke one word all the way—it was at least a half-hour walk. When we got there, he asked me out [for] the next night. I said yes to get rid of him. We went to see an Errol Flynn picture. When we got home, he said, 'I will ask you once more. Will you marry me?' All of a sudden, I said yes. He didn't believe what he heard, so he said, 'What?' I repeated it, and he just took off without a good night."

Floyd came back the next night with "papers galore" for Betty's mother to sign. Soon Betty got a request to appear at U.S. Army head-quarters in the area. "The questions they asked were really something. The main one I got mad at was 'What are you getting married for? Are you pregnant, or what?' Then they asked Floyd the same question, and where he planned on living, England or the U.S.A. He said the U.S.A. We got permission but had to wait six months. Then they shipped him out to Germany in hopes he would change his mind."

They set their wedding date for April 25, 1945. All the invitations went out, the cake was made—and Floyd couldn't get leave. So they had to change the date to May 5. The night of May 4, Betty didn't sleep a wink, worried Floyd wouldn't make it again. He'd been out on maneuvers for forty-eight hours with no sleep, but he arrived for the wedding promptly at six A.M. "We had to fetch the flowers, they wouldn't deliver. We stopped and had a drink. Floyd went to Uncle Fred's house, since we figured it wouldn't look good with us both coming from Mother's, so he and Larry went to the church from there. We arrived at the church a half hour late." A truckload of Italian prisoners, whom the American soldiers were supposed to be guarding, sat outside the church. "The men we'd invited from Floyd's company just left the truck and went into the church. My mother gave me away, and instead of walking slow as we had practiced, we were at the altar before they'd finished playing 'Here Comes the Bride.' We had a high-church wedding in Latin. The only hymn I remember was 'Courage, brother, do not stumble, though thy path be dark as night: There's a star to guide the humble, trust in God.'

"After the wedding, we went into the vestibule and signed the license. When we came out, all the Yanks had rice to throw. Everyone was disgusted, as we hadn't seen rice to *eat* in ages. Then we took pictures outside the church. 'Bloody' is swearing in England, and there was Floyd trying to get everybody lined up, yelling, 'Come on, you bloody Yanks!' From there we went to the Smithfield Hotel for our wedding meal, which was sit-down. Our wedding cake had three tiers, with stars and stripes all over the sides. It was gorgeous and made like prewar, as my boss at work had arranged to get the ingredients to have it made. We had the fifth to get married and the sixth together, and he had to go back on duty on the seventh. He got as far as Southampton, and then the eighth turned out to be VE Day, so he got to come back for a couple of more days."

Once Floyd returned to the army, Betty returned to her usual pattern, working at the co-op during the day and also continuing with the National Fire Service for a while. She saw Floyd for a week in October 1945, but then not again until mid-1946 and her arrival in the United States, where Floyd had settled in New Mexico after his discharge in March of that year.

Betty's journey to America was a taxing one. When she embarked in June, she had to stay at the U.S. Army camp at Tidworth, England, for three days before her ship departed. Her suitcase broke along the way, and she had to borrow a belt to tie around it. "Talk about a poor immigrant," Betty recalls. Along with two hundred other women and some children, Betty crossed the Atlantic on the U.S.S. *Holbrook*, a seven-day voyage with another two days in dock at both ends of the crossing. "It was a miserable trip," she remembers vividly. "First they took us to a room where the captain talked to us. He told us to take seasick pills two or three times a day, but that had us all walking around like zombies, so most of us quit taking them. The ocean was rough, and I was on E Deck, which was below water level with no porthole. Four of us slept on bunk beds in a small cabin—one girl was going to New York, another to Minnesota, and a third to Utah. We stuck together all the time. The shower used salt water, but no one told us, and even though they gave us a special soap, it did nothing for the hair. The Red Cross and other officials had regular showers, but we weren't allowed to use them. We weren't allowed to talk to the crew, and to stop us from going up on A Deck after a certain hour, MPs were posted.

"We would sit on deck all day, with numbers pinned to our clothes. They would call the numbers when it was your turn to eat. Most of the time it was lamb stew for dinner. Whoever got down to the galley first would yell back up what there was to eat, and we'd all groan. Breakfast consisted of eggs with green yolks, bacon that seemed to have a box of salt on every strip, cereal if you wanted it, and coffee. We begged for tea but didn't get it. We were able to buy boxes of candy, though, and we'd share those. I would make sandwiches out of celery."

In addition to not having any decent food to eat, the girls endured some nasty comments from others on the ship. "One day the Red Cross had a style show for us. They told us all their clothes came from New York. They also said our in-laws probably wouldn't be happy to see us, so we all had a chip on our shoulder by the time we reached New York," Betty remembers.

Once the boat docked in New York, those met by their husbands were allowed off right away. Betty and her new friends, though, had another twenty-four hours to wait on board. They couldn't wait to get hold of something they could eat, so they quickly worked out a barter system with dockworkers. "They threw us doughnuts, we threw them cigarettes. The crew tried to stop us, but we did it anyway. Two of us even managed to sneak upstairs to the Red Cross cabins and take a real shower.

"Finally they put us on buses to Hoboken, New Jersey. There we got on a train. We were in the last coach and were shuttled from train to train as we crossed the country. People in the cars in front knew we were there, so they'd come back to peek at us. We finally got to say, 'Come on in and look at the monkeys.' One girl on her way to Seattle had twins. She was supposed to have the one compartment on the train. But they made her stay in a regular berth and the Red Cross women took the compartment, so we all took turns watching her kids so she could get some rest. We ate in the dining coach and were given corn on the cob. We tried cutting it, but that didn't work. So we picked it up and bit into it, and it was awful. No one told us we were supposed to put salt and butter on it."

The car with Betty and the other war brides was switched from train to train during the night, a noisy process that of course woke everyone up. After four long days and interrupted nights, an exhausted Betty finally reached Albuquerque, New Mexico. As the train neared its destination, Betty looked out and saw slums and dilapidated mud huts. "I thought, 'My God, what have I done!' I was the only one getting off. Floyd came running up, all 250 pounds of him. He'd weighed 195 when I'd last seen him. His mother was there, too. On the platform, there were many Indians, the women with papooses on their backs, selling baskets and pots. Talk about culture shock. The local Red Cross officials came over to interview me. I told the truth, that we were treated like prisoners and that the food had been horrible. They got angry, and my arrival wasn't written up in the paper after all; it was supposed to be, since I was the first GI bride to arrive in New Mexico."

Like quite a number of other war brides, Betty felt shell-shocked by her new situation. When she met her new mother-in-law, the first thing she said to Betty was "You're skinny and need fattening up." Floyd's brother George seemed a little weird but friendly. But Betty took an instant liking to her father-in-law when he came home from work at a grocery store. "He called me Betsy and gave me a big hug and a kiss, and I thought he was wonderful.

"Floyd had told me there were certain words I shouldn't say, but he didn't tell me I shouldn't have a drink." So when her father-in-law, who asked her to call him Dad, offered a beer, Betty accepted. No other woman in the group that evening had one. "My first mistake."

To make matters more uncomfortable, the meal her mother-in-law served didn't make Betty think she was going to get "fattened up" any time soon. She had to eat corn on the cob again, although at least Floyd showed her how to eat it properly this time. The mashed potatoes had lumps in them, just like her own mother's, so at least that seemed familiar. But she couldn't quite stomach the white gravy that went with the steak—a southwestern tradition she realized would definitely take some getting used to. When she caught sight of the cottage cheese, which she'd never encountered, she couldn't help but think it "looked like someone had already eaten it." After declining everything except the corn with a polite "no thank you," Betty resigned herself to the fact that "my first meal was a flop. I didn't make a good impression."

After supper, she and Floyd drove twenty-five miles to the house he had rented in Bernalillo. The three-room house contained a living room with a linoleum floor and a hide-a-bed, a second room with a table and some chairs, and a kitchen with an icebox, a two-burner hot plate, and "a kind of oven that fit over a burner." There was no running water, and that was the least of the hardships. "I asked to go to the toilet, and Floyd grabbed a shotgun and took me outside. He had whitewashed the hut and Purexed the seat, but I had never seen an outdoor toilet before. By then I was really shocked. All I heard from the Yanks in England was how backward we were and how modern America was. But at home I had an electric stove and running water in the house, plus a fireplace in every room."

It didn't help to learn that Floyd had brought out the shotgun to keep away the rattlesnakes. He also warned Betty not to leave her shoes on the floor, and to shake them and her clothes before putting them on to make sure no scorpions or black-widow spiders had attached themselves. When she woke up in the middle of the night and turned on the light, she saw bugs scurry all over the ceiling for cover.

Fortunately, Betty and Floyd did not stay long in Bernalillo, a town that consisted of three blocks of wooden sidewalks, a bus depot, a small department store, a tavern with spittoons and sawdust on the floor, a do-it-yourself laundry, and one doctor—"the drunken kind you see in old cowboy movies." Betty still hasn't forgotten how out of place she felt. "I was pure white, like a sheet, and everyone else—even the whites—were brown, so I stood out like a sore thumb."

In midsummer, Floyd's parents decided to move to Washington State, where they hoped to find better jobs. They expected Floyd and Betty to follow, but instead the newlyweds went to Kansas City, Missouri, where Larry Turner, the friend who had introduced them in England and been best man at their wedding, lived. Floyd got a job at the A&P for $35 a week, and Betty was hired at $40 a week by Wolferman's, an elite grocery and wine store run by Englishmen.

Neither of them liked Kansas City all that much, so after six months, they decided to join Floyd's folks in Washington after all. They blew the rods on their 1937 Packard on the way and had to stop to add oil every few miles. "When we came to Chinook Pass, it had just opened, and it was icy. I remember us stopping at the top, me with my foot on the brake, crying, and Floyd adding more oil."

They finally made it to Auburn, Washington, where Betty soon had more new adventures with nature, American-style. At least the house they rented was a step up from their abode in Bernalillo, with two bedrooms, a bathroom, and an eat-in kitchen. But one day they heard splashing coming from the bathroom and rushed in to discover a large rat swimming around in the toilet. Floyd ran next door to ask what to do, and his neighbor instructed him to just flush it back down—which, surprisingly, worked. For years after, Betty checked any new toilet she encountered to make sure it wasn't harboring a rat.

Shortly after they moved to Kent, Washington, Betty experienced her first earthquake. Pregnant at the time with their daughter, Juanita, she had walked across the street to the A&P where Floyd worked. She'd just gotten inside when the whole store began to shake. "Everything was falling off the shelves. The store rolled, and I stood there laughing. 'Run, you damned limey,' Floyd yelled." He broke the lock on the back door so they could get out of the store, but it wasn't much better outside, where cars rolled back and forth across the parking lot.

They survived the ordeal, though, and after a little while in Washington, Floyd heard of some job openings with the border patrol in Albuquerque. He got into shape, dieting back down to 195 pounds, and he and Betty returned to New Mexico. When they got there, they found to their dismay that federal jobs had been abruptly frozen. So he got a position instead as a traveling salesman for Campbell's soup. After seven months, they decided to head northwest to Washington again.

In 1953, Floyd got a sales job with Rainier Brewery. At long last, he and Betty and Juanita settled down for good. Floyd worked for Rainier for thirty-five years, until his retirement.

Betty Law Bachman wrote this account of the war years and her early experiences in America before her death in a car accident in 1998. Her daughter, Juanita, now adds that Betty lived a rewarding and happy life. "She put in over forty thousand hours of volunteer work at the VA hospital, working mostly with the blind in later years. She served the VFW auxiliary on the local, state, and national level. She also joined and became active in the local chapter of the Daughters of the British Empire. My parents vastly improved their standard of living from the early outhouse days. Mother went 'home' many times to visit family, although she said it was never the same after her mother died. She always referred to England as home and never lost her British accent and traditions, yet she was as American and patriotic as they come. She was very proud to be a naturalized citizen."

So, despite the shock of finding out that America wasn't quite the dreamy landscape she'd imagined, Betty ended up embracing life with her American husband in her new country with open arms.

The wallet photographs that Betty and Floyd exchanged to remember each other before she came to the United States.

Betty, Floyd, and their wedding party.

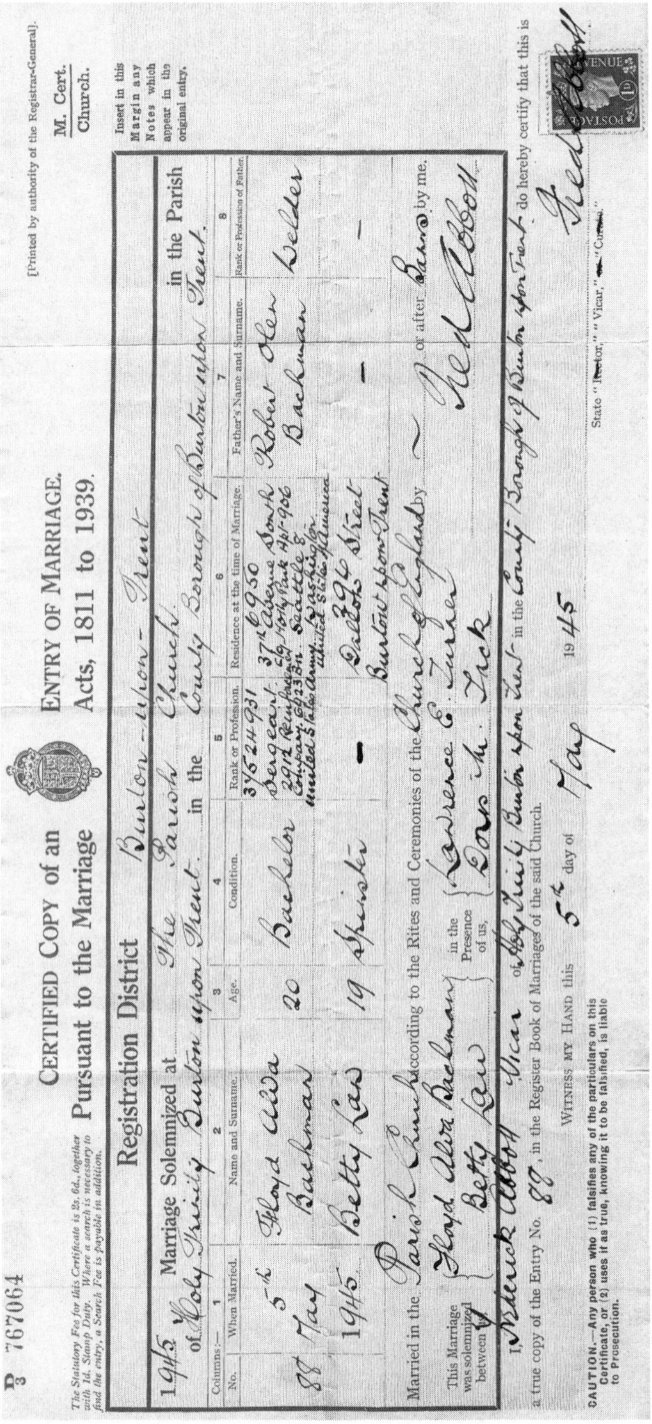

B 3 767064

The Statutory Fee for this Certificate is 2s. 6d., together with 1d. Stamp Duty. Where a search is necessary to find the entry, a Search Fee is payable in addition.

CERTIFIED COPY of an ENTRY OF MARRIAGE.
Pursuant to the Marriage Acts, 1811 to 1939.

[Printed by authority of the Registrar-General].

M. Cert. Church.

Registration District Burton-upon-Trent

1945 Marriage Solemnized at The Parish Church in the Parish of Holy Trinity Burton upon Trent in the County Borough of Burton upon Trent.

| No. | When Married. | Name and Surname. | Age. | Condition. | Rank or Profession. | Residence at the time of Marriage. | Father's Name and Surname. | Rank or Profession of Father. |
|---|---|---|---|---|---|---|---|---|
| 88 | 5th Jan 1945 | Floyd Alva Bachman | 20 | Bachelor | 37524931 Sergeant 2912 Reinforcement Company, 6023 Bn. United States Army | 37th 6950 Avenue South c/o 4014 Park A.P.O. 906 Seattle 8 Washington United States of America | Robert Olen Bachman | Welder |
| | | Betty Law | 19 | Spinster | — | 296 Dalton Street Burton upon Trent | — | — |

Married in the Parish Church according to the Rites and Ceremonies of the Church of England by ~ or after Banns by me.

This Marriage was solemnized between us, Floyd Alva Bachman, Betty Law; in the Presence of us, Lawrence E. Turner, Doris M. Tuck; Fred Abbott.

I, Frederick Abbott Vicar of Holy Trinity Burton upon Trent in the County Borough of Burton upon Trent do hereby certify that this is a true copy of the Entry No. 88, in the Register Book of Marriages of the said Church.

Witness my Hand this 5th day of May 1945. Fred Abbott

State "Rector," "Vicar," or "Curate."

Insert in this Margin any Notes which appear in the original entry.

CAUTION.—Any person who (1) falsifies any of the particulars on this Certificate, or (2) uses it as true, knowing it to be falsified, is liable to Prosecution.

*Betty and Floyd's English wedding license.*

*Betty on board the U.S.S.* Holbrook, *making her way to the U.S.*

*Betty, Floyd, and their daughter, Juanita Bachman Brunzell, in the spring of 1950 in Washington State.*

*Betty Law Bachman in 1997, the year before her death.*

WHEN AN AMERICAN SERVICEMAN
*fell in love with a young woman he
met in a foreign country, the reactions
of the girl's family varied greatly. In a recently liber-
ated country, such an alliance was often considered a
godsend, offering the daughter a much better life in
America. Marriage under such circumstances might
be actively facilitated by the family. In other cases,
however, the overtures of an American serviceman
were deeply resented and resisted by the family. Such
reactions were particularly common in England, where
feelings against "crass" upstart Americans still lingered
from World War I days. A young woman had to be
quite courageous to go through with a wedding that
might well lead to a permanent breach with a parent.*

*Max McClure in the cockpit of his P-47 fighter plane.*
*Ena McClure in 1945.*

# *Max and Ena*
## McCLURE

In the last week of May 1943, Ena King's good friend Rosemary telephoned her in London and asked her to go on a blind date. Her American pilot friend was coming into town on an R&R leave, and another pilot, a buddy of his, was coming with him. Ena declined. She wasn't interested in going on a blind date, and she had heard some unpleasant things about American servicemen. The British generally had mixed feelings about the Americans living among them. They certainly recognized that the participation of the American forces was crucial to winning the war. But while the good-humored brashness of so many American GIs appealed to some Brits, especially young women, it rankled others. That was especially true for the young men who were losing so many dates to their American counterparts. Many British soldiers warned their sisters about the dangers of what they saw as "love 'em and leave 'em" affairs.

But when Ena turned down the date, her friend Rosemary leaned on her, telling her what a spoilsport she was. She also promised Ena that she wouldn't be left alone with the mystery man. Not wanting to disappoint her friend, Ena finally gave in when Rosemary asked a fourth time.

The date proved to be pleasant enough but nothing special, just dinner at a place that also had a dance floor. The day before had been Ena's birthday, and her brother had bought her a stunning red suit that she wore that night, setting off her black hair beautifully. Ena's date, Max McClure from Texas, was very handsome, but he wasn't much of a dancer, which was a real drawback during those dance-crazed times.

Even though she felt no special sparks during the date, when Max dropped her off at home, he asked her for her phone number. She didn't expect to hear from him again, but just in case—rather than give him her home number and risk her family discovering she'd dated an American—she gave him her work number at Mogashel Linens, the high-quality store where she was a receptionist.

The very next week, Max called to say he was coming to London again and asked her to dinner and the theater. She started warming to him on that second date, possibly because they were both more relaxed. She began to perceive the intelligence behind his Texan drawl. Over the next few weeks, Max traveled up to London to see Ena as often as possible. He was a P-47 fighter pilot in the 358th Fighter Group, and he escorted the bombers on their missions to France and Germany. Because he had volunteered to stay on for a second tour, after having flown the fifty missions that made a full tour, he was allowed to leave his base when he was not scheduled to fly.

On their dates, he and Ena would have a nice meal and go either to the theater or, more often, the movies. She particularly remembers going to see Irene Dunne in the tearjerker *The White Cliffs of Dover*, and how moved they both were. That afternoon, she remembers, while they were walking through Leicester Square, a young woman suddenly called out, "Hello, Max, how are you?" Max looked around hurriedly, didn't answer, and pulled Ena along so quickly that she didn't even get a look at the woman. Taken aback by his abruptness, Ena asked Max who the woman was and why he was so rude to her. He replied simply, "You don't want to know her." Suddenly she thought that Max might have another life she knew nothing about. Ena says that Max never again brought up the encounter, and she never pressed him about it. Sometimes things were better left unexplored, and, after all, Max had chosen to be with her. During the war years, it was almost a rule not to question soldiers too closely about their romantic past. There were almost always old girlfriends, and life had become very present-tense. Everyone was uprooted in some way, and the future was always uncertain.

One night when Max came up to London, they went to see the movie *A Yank in the RAF*, a piece of wartime froth starring Tyrone Power, Betty Grable, and the English actor John Sutton, who was a particular favorite of Ena's. Originally released three years earlier, in 1941, the picture seemed to be playing at one or another theater almost continually, like many popular films of the period. After the movie, Max took Ena home on the bus, which was their usual means of transportation. At eighteen, Ena was the baby of her family, with two older brothers and an older sister, and she lived with her parents. Just after Max and Ena got off the bus, air-raid sirens began blaring, followed by the "ack-ack" of anti-aircraft artillery. They began to hurry, and then Max abruptly stopped walking, turned to Ena, and asked her to marry him. In the midst of all those ominous sounds of war, she looked into Max's face, full of anticipation, and realized that she had fallen in love with him. She said yes immediately. When she is asked today what it was about Max that particularly attracted her, she says, "Everything. He was the one for me. I knew it."

As soon as Max left her at her door that night, she burst into the house and rushed excitedly to her parents' bedroom, announcing, "Mommy, Max has asked me to marry him!" Ena's father was an extremely sound sleeper; even air-raid sirens usually didn't wake him. But the moment Ena's momentous news was out of her mouth, her father sat bolt upright in bed and said, "Go to your room, turn off the light, and I don't want that American in this house ever again!" Nobody in the family ever disagreed with Ena's father. He was a tough disciplinarian, and she had rarely seen him so intense. She was stunned and crushed by his reaction, and she went to her room in despair.

But Ena was a determined young woman. She continued to see Max surreptitiously, despite her father's continuing opposition. Her mother approved but was not about to try to change her husband's mind. He was not the kind of man to enter into debate with either his wife or his children.

Sometime later, the weekend after D-Day, Ena went down to see Max in High Halden, Kent, where he was stationed. The land on which the airbase had been constructed was owned by Lady Morris, who had been allowed to remain in her beautiful home on the base. Max was friendly with her, often buying eggs from her, which were a precious commodity. He asked Lady Morris if Ena could stay with her for the weekend, and she agreed. Not the least snobbish or aloof, Lady Morris was very kind to Ena, welcoming her to the base for Max because he was out flying a mission. When he returned later that day, Ena and he went off on a picnic.

The base was in what was known as "buzzbomb country," a repeated target of German V1 rockets. Ena was used to falling bombs in London, the major target of the Battle of Britain, which still continued to be bombed sporadically. Like most Britons, she had learned to be fatalistic about bombs. You never knew when they might come, and if you thought about it much, you would be too afraid ever to leave your home. Even so, the countryside was so peaceful as they enjoyed their picnic that Ena was shocked to hear anti-aircraft guns fired nearby. "I nearly climbed a tree," Ena recalls.

Early the next morning, Max came to Lady Morris's house to tell Ena that his fighter group was leaving for France. He asked her to come to the end of the runway to watch them leave. As she stood there, surrounded by menacing barbed wire, she watched Max and the rest of his group take off one by one. She wondered how many of them would come back, and if she would ever see Max again, and her eyes filled with tears.

She did see Max again, but not for several weeks. In late August she went to see him at his new base in Atchem, near Shrewsbury, almost all the way to the Welsh border. He was approaching a hundred missions and the end of his second tour of duty. Not only was Max farther away now, but they knew they had to face some difficult decisions because he would soon be rotated back to the U.S. They decided to marry.

Though Ena's father was still strongly opposed to the relationship, Ena's mother felt differently. Her own marriage had been arranged, and she was determined that Ena should marry for love, so she signed the papers that allowed Ena to marry. Ena King and Max Whitely McClure were married at Shrewsbury on November 3, 1944.

Ena knew her father wouldn't attend, but he also forbade her mother to go. Since her mother had enraged her father by signing the marriage papers, Ena knew her mother was in no position to defy him further, but she was deeply hurt that her mother couldn't be there. The choice she had been forced to make between Max and her father was agonizing.

Ena and Max spent their honeymoon at a hotel called the Mytton & Mermaid. Then, just three days later, Max returned to the U.S. Ena's father was so angry about the marriage that he told her she was no longer his daughter. She had to move out of the house and live with her older sister. She would not see Max again for ten months.

Max had not described his hometown of Spur, Texas, in much detail. His father had founded the town newspaper in 1909 and the McClures had stayed happily rooted in Spur ever since. The town was tiny, he had warned her, even smaller than the smallest English village Max had seen. Ena's sister, on hearing this, said, "I give you three weeks there." But Ena was not worried. Receiving the word from Max that he was back home and ready for her to come over, she booked herself onto a Norwegian cargo ship that left England on August 31, 1945, paying her own way. Max wired her that he would be waiting for her in New York at the dock.

Max had bought chocolates and flowers for their hotel room and couldn't wait until she stepped off that ship. But when he called the shipping line on the day she was to arrive, to confirm the time of arrival, he discovered that the ship had been diverted to Baltimore. During the war, such diversions were common due to the war-related sea traffic. Now Max had to drive frantically down to Maryland, and he sent Ena a telegram to assure her he was on the way.

The ship docked in the shadow of Fort McHenry, celebrated in "The Star-Spangled Banner." The day was September 13, 1945, the 131st anniversary of the British naval bombardment of Fort McHenry in the War of 1812, and the harbor was bursting with fireworks as the ship came into port. Once she'd disembarked, Ena asked a nearby policeman what the fireworks were all about, and he answered, "This is the day we celebrate our liberation from the British." Such was her welcome to the United States.

When Ena arrived in Spur, she discovered the town was just as tiny as Max had warned, but also that it was a wonderfully friendly place. The whole town welcomed her like a long-lost relative. After all, she had married Max McClure, the returning war hero. After a period of adjustment to the American way of life, Ena settled down into a very happy routine in Spur. She wrote to her family often and received many letters back, but the rift between her and her father remained painful.

Then, in 1948, Ena's mother came to visit. Although she fully acknowledged how contented Ena and Max were together, and was pleased to find Ena as happy as she'd led them to believe, she nonetheless conveyed a distressing message from Ena's father: Unless Ena returned to England, he would consider her dead. After all this time, he still couldn't bring himself to accept that she'd "run off" with an American. There was no question about Ena's response: She told her mother to let her father know that she was deeply in love with Max and was very happy where she was.

Over the next two years, Ena's family worked on convincing her father that he had to accept Ena's marriage and make his peace with her. Finally, he consented to invite Ena to England for a visit, and he promised that he would join the rest of the family in meeting her at the train station in London. Ena made the crossing on the luxurious *Queen Mary* and took the train from Southampton to London. All the way over, she had felt more and more anxiety, mixed with anticipation, about the reunion with her father. After all of that, when she looked out on the platform, bursting with the excitement of seeing her family for the first time in years, she was stunned to discover that her father was not there. How could he have failed to come?

Deeply disappointed, she walked up to her family. "Where's your father?" her mother asked. "Not with me!" Ena replied in surprise. Her father, it turned out, had decided that he would meet Ena as she got off the ship in Southampton, then take the train with her up to London to meet the rest of them. Somehow, he had missed her there, and they learned what had happened only when he showed up in London three hours later.

After Ena had been home for several days, her father asked her to come into his study one afternoon. She went in and closed the door, not knowing what to expect. Her father asked her if she loved Max, and she replied that she did, very much. He asked her if she was happy with her life with Max, and she told him she was, very. "Very well, then," he said, "we won't talk about this again." Many years later, Max and Ena spent three years in London, during which time Ena's father got to know Max well and discovered that he quite liked his American son-in-law.

Despite the separation from her family, Ena McClure says in reflecting on her life with Max, "I was very lucky." She recalls that one day, during their fifty-first year of marriage, Max looked across the room at her and suddenly said, "Once I was this dashing fighter pilot, and I went to England and met a beautiful girl with black hair. She was wearing a red suit with white cuffs. And I fell in love." She had never known that he had remembered so vividly what she had been wearing on that fateful day.

Ena enjoyed fifty-one years and seven months of a wonderful marriage and love affair with a dashing P-47 fighter pilot from Spur, Texas. Major Max McClure passed away June 7, 1996, and is buried at Fort Sam Houston National Cemetery in San Antonio.

**"THE MYTTON & MERMAID"**
**Atcham, Shrewsbury**
*Telephone :* CROSS HOUSES 220
HALFWAY HOUSE TO PORTMEIRION

View of Hotel through the gateway to Attingham Park

*A brochure for the Mytton & Mermaid, where Ena and Max spent their honeymoon.*

*Ena and Max on the front steps of his mother's house shortly after Ena arrived in Spur.*

*Ena and Max attending a formal at Web Air Force Base in 1953.*

*Ena and Max on one of many trips to England, in 1962.*

B EGINNING IN ITALY IN LATE 1943, *then continuing across northern Europe through 1944 and 1945, American soldiers came as liberators. People who had suffered a great deal and lost much met them with joy and gratitude. The Americans brought a promise of eventual peace, of normal lives resumed, of days no longer consumed by fear. Sometimes they also brought the promise of love. Fulfilling that promise could bring about even more profound change for those who had already suffered so much. Was the love strong enough to make the separation from family, friends, and country worthwhile? These were difficult decisions to make, even in a world restored to peace.*

*Harold and Jeanne Conn as newlyweds.*

# *Harold and Jeanne*
## CONN

Jeanne Cuvelier was born in her maternal grandmother's house on February 23, 1927, in Adinkerke–De Panne, Belgium. She grew up in Brussels, where, she remembers, she had a very happy childhood. During school vacations, she and her brother Jean, who was eighteen months older, would visit their grandparents. "Grandmom would take all eight of her grandchildren and her dog to the dunes, where we would play all afternoon long," Jeanne remembers.

On May 10, 1940, the Germans invaded Belgium, and thirteen-year old Jeanne's dreamy, peaceful childhood came to an end.

"Lots of bridges and train stations were destroyed early on," Jeanne recalls. "We were not allowed to travel by train any farther than Ghent, so we did not see our grandparents. My parents bought a tandem bicycle to ride out and see their folks every few months. It was during that awful time that my grandfather died of a heart attack on the street, carrying a heavy bag of coal bought on the black market. My brother and I weren't allowed to go to his funeral. My parents rode their bike."

The strict rules set down by the Germans put a considerable strain on people trying to push their fear aside and get on with their daily lives. "There was a curfew, and adults needed special passes to be outdoors late at night. There was a complete blackout ordered, and we could be arrested if any light was seen through windows or doors. In the beginning there was no music allowed, and dancing was forbidden in the cafés. We were heavily rationed, and there was little food available, anyway. We would have to stand in line for hours in front of a fish store to be able to buy a couple of smoked herrings for a family of four. Toward the end of the month, we would just throw away our food stamps because the stores didn't have enough merchandise to supply everyone. Clothes and shoes were unavailable. People knitted sweaters and skirts when they were able to find some yarn somewhere."

Jeanne had elected to go to a French-speaking high school instead of a Flemish one (both languages are spoken in Belgium). Since her family spoke Flemish at home, she hoped to perfect her lesser command of French.

Soon, however, the Gestapo arrived to check the school records. Any student with Flemish roots was told they must go to a Flemish school. Luckily, the school administrators found a way around the rule. They hired a couple of young Flemish teachers and turned a large supply room into a classroom. "The Flemish department was formed, and the 'L'Ecole Professionelle Marius Renard' became bilingual. Since there were only five girls in my class, it was almost like private tutoring, and we received a fabulous high school education."

With the invasion of Normandy in June 1944, a new struggle for the control of Belgium developed. Jeanne remains deeply grateful to this day for the bravery of the American soldiers during the bloody Battle of the Bulge in eastern Belgium and Luxembourg, when "so many offered up their lives to liberate the Allied countries."

After the Americans and British finally pushed the German troops back out of Belgium, only the British troops were commonly seen in Brussels. "It wasn't until October or November that we started seeing a few American soldiers in Brussels for R&R. There were now large dance halls and clubs for the Allied military. We Belgian girls could get a membership card to participate in entertaining the troops. There were two bands, a continental British orchestra and a great American band. It took us no time to learn to do the boogie-woogie with GIs. After more than four years of restriction, we could dance again!

"On February 18, 1945, I accompanied a friend of mine whose mother ran a café. That's where I met a very nice and polite GI whose name was Harold Conn, but he was called 'H' for short. I had never heard of such a name. As I was about to leave, he insisted on walking me home. At the time, I was working for the Kredietbank downtown, and we made plans to meet again the next day in front of the Metropole Hotel."

After a few more encounters with "H," Jeanne took him in to meet her family after he walked her home one evening. It wasn't at all unusual for people to welcome soldiers into their homes in those days.

Jeanne celebrated her eighteenth birthday five days after she met Harold; he had his twenty-fifth three days after that. He was transferred to Antwerp in April to work on the docks, operating a crane to unload the big ships bringing in supplies for the Allied forces. Even so, he became Jeanne's steady date. "My father had already told me that it was 'out of the question' for me to become 'one of those war brides,' so anything serious seemed just a pipe dream. H [as she came to call him] was discharged at the end of November 1945. He made his way to France and then home to Pennsylvania just in time for Christmas."

Jeanne got a telegram from Hal that Christmas. She hadn't expected to hear from him again, but they corresponded for nineteen months. During that time, Hal proceeded to get the necessary papers for her to come to America. Jeanne very much wanted to go, and finally her father relented. After all, she was a young woman now, and she'd had nearly two years to decide it was what she wanted.

Unlike the war brides, who were brought to America at government expense, Jeanne had to pay for her own transportation. Women in her position were given only ninety-day visas to the United States. If they had not gotten married by the end of that period, they had to leave the country.

"On June 27, 1947, I left Brussels by Sabena Airlines to La Guardia Airport in New York City," Jeanne recalls. "It took sixteen hours with three refueling stops. When Hal picked me up at the airport, there were problems with immigration. Hal was supposed to have posted a $500 bond to cover my return expenses should we fail to marry in ninety days. This forced a twenty-four-hour stay at Ellis Island until Hal could get to the bank and post the bond. Luckily, his grandfather lived in New York and was able to help. After that adventure, we boarded a train for Philadelphia. Hal's mom welcomed me with open arms, and we became friends right away. I was very fortunate. Hal and I were married on July 10, 1947, and our first and only child, James, was born on July 2, 1948."

James gave Jeanne her own taste of what it can be like to lose a child to a foreign place. When Jim was a teenager, he decided to enter the priesthood. Jeanne had as hard a time with his decision as her own father had with her choice to go to America. Not only did Jim's choice mean she would never have grandchildren, but she feared that he would end up far away from home. "For the first time," she recollects, "I felt homesick, thinking about my parents and how hard it must have been for them to let me go to live so very far away."

But Father James J. Conn, SJ, has made her very proud. "He's a canon lawyer with a doctorate from the Pontifical Gregorian University in Rome, a civil law degree from Fordham University in New York, and is a member of the Maryland bar. He is currently a professor of canon law at the Gregorian University." Jeanne and Hal Conn celebrated their fifty-third wedding anniversary in Philadelphia, Pennsylvania, in July 2000.

*Harold and Jeanne in front of her parents' house in Brussels in 1945.*

*Studio portraits of Harold and Jeanne, both taken in 1945.*

*Harold and Jeanne on their fiftieth wedding anniversary with their son, Reverend James J. Conn, SJ.*

AMID THE RUBBLE AND DEPRIVATION *of countries devastated by the war, first in Italy, and later France, Belgium, Holland, and ultimately Germany itself, American soldiers offered vital assistance. Sometimes a kind response to a request for help was all it took to make sparks fly across cultures. Most of the European women whom the soldiers met didn't speak English, but in such circumstances, especially, a look or a touch of the hand can speak volumes.*

*Anna Della Casa Gonzales in 1944.*

# Anna Della Casa

## GONZALES

Born in Naples, Italy, in 1926, Anna Della Casa survived a number of hair-raising adventures before coming to America as a war bride. Now living in San Bruno, California, near San Francisco, she tells her remarkable story with great verve and good humor, taking understandable pride in the fact that she did not meet her GI husband at a Red Cross or USO tea party or dance, but in the midst of a dangerous war-torn city. Only pluck and pure luck kept her alive until the day that Private John Gonzales entered her young life.

Anna was born a middle child in a Neapolitan family of sixteen girls and two boys. She says she wasn't scared when she heard people talking about the impending war, but once it started, she was scared all the time.

Anna experienced plenty of deprivation during the first three years of the war, but things got much worse when the Americans invaded Italy. The coming of the Americans didn't frighten the Italians very much—by that time, Americans were widely welcomed, as they provided hope that the Germans might one day be defeated. The Italians worried instead about the remaining presence of the German military on the mainland, ruthless troops whose job it was to thwart the American advance for as long as possible, and who regarded Italians with cruel contempt. The Pact of Steel alliance that Italy's fascist dictator Benito Mussolini had signed with Adolf Hitler in May 1939 brought little to the country but grief, and as time wore on, the German high command's increasing disdain for Mussolini funneled into a hatred of the ordinary Italian soldier. In turn, the Italian people came to hate the Germans, and as their dictator became increasingly unhinged, they understood that their salvation depended almost wholly on the success of the Allied invasion.

Many Italians also had relatives who had emigrated to the United States, so they felt a far greater sense of connection to America than to Germany. Berlin and Munich certainly had no "Little Italy" neighborhoods, as so many American cities did and still do.

The American, British, and Canadian forces began their invasion of Italy in Sicily on July 10, 1943. By the sixteenth, they had made sufficient headway for Prime Minister Winston Churchill and President Franklin D. Roosevelt to issue a joint statement calling for the surrender of Italy. They backed up that call with bombing raids on Rome and subsequently Naples. The bombardment of Naples was devastating, and Anna vividly remembers the terror of three days she spent in an air raid shelter during an intense period of bombing. The shelter was in an ancient tunnel under the city, built by the Romans during the days when Pompeii was a flourishing city on the Bay of Naples. Anna huddled in the shelter with some three hundred others and heard the crash of the building above them collapsing from what must have been a direct hit.

On July 25, the Grand Council of the Fascist party arrested Mussolini and replaced him with Marshal Pietro Badoglio. The replacement paved the way for the Italian surrender, signed in Sicily on September 3. Five days later, the surrender was officially announced to the world, after the Allies had already begun to invade the Italian mainland.

The Nazi forces continued to fight the Allies in Italy. During the fighting on Sicily, forty thousand German troops escaped to the mainland, augmenting their considerable presence there. The Nazi forces fought with such ferocity during the ensuing months that it took almost a year for the Allies to penetrate as far north as Florence.

While the American and British forces invaded mainland Italy in three places—Reggio at the toe of Italy's boot, Taranto on the inner heel, and Salerno, south of Naples—the Germans took control of Rome. They did not fully control Naples, but Anna Della Casa Gonzales remembers all too well that it felt like "they were everywhere." During this period, when she was eighteen, she had two frightening encounters with German troops.

American bombs had disrupted the water supply in the part of the city where she lived, so one day her mother dispatched her with a pail to get some water at the waterfront. "I complained, of course," Anna recalls. "But Mama said, 'Go.'" On the way, Anna heard a commotion and saw a crowd gathered in front of a delicatessen. Voices called out, "Free food! Free food!" Some German soldiers had broken in the door of the shop and were shouting at people, telling them to take whatever they wanted. Food was difficult to find in Naples, so a number of people rushed in, including Anna, who filled her pail with flour instead of water and grabbed a salami.

Just as she was about to run out, she saw the men shot dead right in front of her as they left the shop, by the same German soldiers who had broken down the door. Anna quickly realized she was caught in a cruel trap. As fast as she could, she made her way back through the shop and found a rear window big enough to crawl through. She then moved cautiously through the back streets of Naples, taking the most roundabout route home, so as not to be seen or followed.

Word of the shooting incident spread instantly all across town. Someone had seen Anna go into the shop with her pail, and told her horrified mother that Anna had never come out. When Anna rushed to her mother's side, having safely navigated a route home, calling, "Mama, I got some flour," her mother took one look and keeled over in a faint.

Shortly after her first face-to-face encounter with the cruelty of the German soldiers, she faced another situation that put her survival skills and bravery to an even greater test. One afternoon, a group of German soldiers rounded up and carted away her teenage brother and a couple of other boys. Everyone wrote them off for dead. The Italians knew that the Germans, now their official enemies, often shot teenage Italian boys who might otherwise grow to take up arms against them. They liked to make a vicious sport of it, taking the boys to the edge of the city, tying them to trees, and using them for target practice.

Anna had an older male cousin who owned a small truck. She and a couple of family friends piled into it and drove out to an area they knew the Germans favored for their deadly games. Sure enough, there were her brother and the two other boys tied to trees. The German soldiers were out of sight, although Anna and her friends could hear them a little way off in a wooded area.

To create a distraction, Anna ran down the road a few hundred yards, stood by some bushes where she couldn't be seen, and started screaming at the top of her lungs. After a couple of minutes, she heard the voices of the soldiers quickly coming toward her. As the soldiers searched for the source of her screams, her friends quickly freed the three boys. All except Anna clambered into the back of the truck and roared down the road just in time to grab her, now running for her life, as the Germans hit the road where she had stood. "We all got away safe!" Anna exclaims. "No one hurt!" She laughs, but even now there is a hint of breathlessness in her voice.

Anna and her family were immensely relieved when American soldiers took up temporary residence at the University of Naples, across the street from their house. Anna's new American neighbors proved very friendly. One day in September, Anna stood outside her house holding her niece, the daughter of an older sister who had been killed when an American bomb hit her house. The child and Anna's brother-in-law lived with Anna's family now. The family next door to Anna's house had arranged to do laundry for the soldiers, and this day, when a group came to pick up their laundry, one of the soldiers, John Gonzales, struck up a friendly conversation with Anna and her brother-in-law. A few days later, when some of the soldiers in John's company came by, they told Anna that John was interested in marrying her, and she told them to stop teasing her, adding, with her innate Neapolitan cheekiness, "If he likes me so much, tell him to get some food for this baby."

John promptly came to her house the next day with an armful of food for the baby. This was no easy task. Anna's family had the money to pay for food; there just wasn't any to buy. John's gift had a significance far greater than the monetary value of the goods he provided. After this, John came to visit often.

The large age gap between Anna and John, nearly twenty years her senior, was not out of the ordinary in Europe at the time. Still, Anna was cautious when John first suggested marriage, and told him she thought they ought to wait a while. John, hoping to encourage her not to put it off for too long, pointed out that he could be posted elsewhere at any time. He also added that his captain had his eye on Anna and might pull rank, which made Anna laugh.

Perhaps it helped that Anna's mother liked John and thought he would make a good husband. Not only would it be nice to have an American soldier in the family, but John also promised to take Anna to America as soon as the war was over. There she would have opportunities unavailable to her in Italy.

So Anna and John were married by a justice of the peace at the end of September 1943. Anna's family tried to persuade their parish priest to conduct a religious service to make the marriage legal in the eyes of the Catholic Church. Fortunately, John was also Catholic, which made things easier, and after weeks of inveigling, the priest agreed to marry them again at the beginning of January.

As it turned out, the religious ceremony took place just in the nick of time. Right after, they found John's captain waiting to deliver the news that the groom must report for duty immediately. His company had been ordered to leave Naples that very afternoon. John and Anna begged the captain to let them attend their wedding reception, at least for a little while, and of course to come join them himself. He agreed but, after just one hour, insisted that he and John leave. A tearful Anna kissed her husband good-bye, with no idea when or if she would ever see him again.

John was among the thirty-four thousand men to land at Anzio on January 22, 1944. Only thirteen soldiers died that day, a relatively small number compared to most days of battle, but John stepped on a mine and was very seriously injured. He barely survived and had to be hospitalized for a year and a half, first in Italy, then back in America. He delayed contacting Anna for a long time. For many months he was in no condition to write anyone, and nobody knew if he would ever recover—and if he did, to what extent. He feared that he would end up an unemployable invalid, hardly the sort of man he could expect a young girl like Anna, who had her whole life ahead of her, to cherish.

Anna, still in Italy, kept trying to obtain information about his whereabouts and condition from the Red Cross in Naples, to little avail. Wives everywhere, even back in America, often hit a brick wall when searching for their wounded husbands. In part, these difficulties arose due to continued security concerns as the war in Europe dragged on. They also occurred because the military bureaucracy was utterly overwhelmed.

Though they couldn't offer her much help, the Red Cross workers were always very nice to Anna and tried to lift her spirits by telling her stories about what it would be like for her to live in America after the war was over. Anna handled the lack of information about her husband with a patience and calm that belied her years. She found the taunts of young Italian men one of the hardest things to deal with. They'd tease her constantly, saying, "I see your wedding ring, but where's your husband?" Anna had no problem talking back to them, and her feisty wit may have saved her the indignity of having her hair cut off, a fate that befell a number of Italian girls who had married American servicemen.

In November 1945, over a year after she received word of his injury, Anna finally heard from John. He wrote to her from a veteran's hospital in Texas, where he was about to be released after nearly twenty months of surgery and recuperation. He told Anna that he was going to San Francisco to live with a sister and her husband, so he could save up some money once he found a job. And he sent her the necessary papers to bring her to the United States to join him.

Anna had never totally lost hope, but it seemed a miracle that, after so long, John should turn out to be still alive. She promptly wrote back to the San Francisco address but heard nothing back. Though she wondered what might be wrong, there were no problems regarding the validity of her papers, so she simply kept writing and preparing for her trip.

Her name headed the list of Italian war brides making the transatlantic crossing in May 1946 on the *Algonquin*. Rough weather at that time of year and very crowded conditions on an old, unrefurbished ship made the crossing quite difficult. Anna gives a kind of verbal shudder as she sums up her memories of the crossing. The storm-battered ship at last arrived, safe and sound, in New York on May 17, which was her birthday.

Anna was supposed to take a train across the country to San Francisco, but as there was a rail strike going on, she and the other war brides had to wait several days on the ship until a special train was commissioned to take them. She managed to send a telegram to John about her change in plans, but since she still hadn't gotten any reply to her earlier letters, she wasn't sure what to expect when she finally made it to San Francisco.

As she'd feared, when she arrived, she saw no sign of John at the station. Another war bride traveling with her kindly insisted that she come and stay with her for the time being. A helpful policewoman then located John at work. She said to him, "Your wife is here."

He replied, "No, my wife is in Italy."

"No, she's here in San Francisco," the officer repeated.

John refused to believe it. By the time he finally showed up to greet Anna, she'd just about given up and was ready to go home to Mama. She was quite angry, but John carefully explained to her that he had not received any of her letters, or her telegram. In fact, he had begun to worry that she had stopped loving him and wasn't going to come to America at all. When he looked at her with earnest tenderness and said, "Anna, I love you," all of her anger and frustration melted.

When Anna and John investigated the matter of the missing letters, they discovered that John's sister had thrown them all away. She thought John's marriage to Anna had been a terrible mistake. She got away with her attempt to sabotage their union for a long period of time, because John worked nights and was always asleep when the mail came.

Despite the sister's animosity, Anna and John had no choice but to stay with her and her husband. They simply didn't have enough money to get a place of their own yet. Anna's brother-in-law always treated her well, which made life bearable. Whenever the two men were absent, though, John's sister continued to give Anna a very hard time. Anna's almost immediate pregnancy put another strain on her relationship with John's sister, as the sister and her husband had been unable to have children. Anna felt uncomfortable during the days, but she made every effort to brighten up when John came home. She tried not to complain too much, since she was so happy being with him.

One day while the men were working, John's sister came into Anna and John's bedroom and told Anna to bring a particular chair downstairs. It was a favorite, she insisted, and she wanted it back. Anna, nine months pregnant, refused. Sitting in that chair was the only way she could be comfortable in her condition. In a fury, Anna's sister-in-law threatened to hit her. Anna wasn't about to let such a threat pass lightly. She had gotten through the war by learning how to deal with a crisis, and for the first time she stood up to her sister-in-law and made it clear she would fight back if necessary. Once she showed her grit, her sister-in-law left her alone.

Soon after the baby was born, Anna and John finally were able to get a place of their own. Anna had four more children over the next years, a total of three girls and two boys. After that, she told herself,

*Anna in Italy in 1944, with an American army truck in the background.*

*Photographs of Anna and John taken after she had arrived in the U.S.*

AMERICAN RED CROSS MEMBERSHIP CARD

for Wives of American Service Men

Mrs. *Anna Gonzales nee Delle Casa*
is invited to the third floor of the Naples Continental
Club at the times scheduled here:
*Monday & Thursday 2:30*

| | | |
|---|---|---|
| Sunday: | 3:30-6:30 | Date Dance |
| Tuesday: | 1:30-2:30 | English Class |
| Wednesday: | 7:30-10:00 | Movie |
| Thursday: | 1:30-2:30 | English Class |
| Friday: | 7:30-10:00 | Movie |
| Saturday: | 1:30-2:30 | English Class |

*1-1944*

(if special programs are planned for other hours, the M.P. at the
club entrance will be notified.)

Signed *Frederick P. Lutz*
Director

*A copy of Anna's Red Cross membership card, listing activities organized for the wives of American servicemen.*

*Anna and John celebrating their fortieth wedding anniversary in January 1984, just months before he passed away in June.*

*Anna (second from left, front row) with a group of war brides at a reunion party in San Mateo, California, on July 31, 1999. The cake is adorned with flags representing all of the countries the brides came from.*

"I'd better stop, I don't want to become like my mama!" One of her sons, tragically, was killed by a drunk driver when he was nineteen. The other four have grown up and given her twenty-five grandchildren and seven great-grandchildren.

John Gonzales lived to be eighty-five, despite his extensive war injuries. "He still looked so young," Anna recalls. One of her granddaughters once said, "I want to have skin like yours," to which Anna replied, "No, you want skin like your grandpa's."

Anna still takes pride in having obtained her American citizenship all by herself in 1949. True, war brides didn't have to wait as long as other immigrants, but Anna worked hard on her English and studied for the test all on her own. After all, she was officially the first Italian war bride to come to the United States, and she felt she had a responsibility to live up to.

W AR BRIDES WERE NOT THE *only ones to experience difficulties due to their romances with American* soldiers; sometimes the soldiers experienced problems of their own. Some had to endure the agony of doubt as they waited for their brides to show up on the special cruises arranged by the government. Others might encounter bureaucratic hassles in making arrangements for the couple to be together again.

*Erwin (Hal) and Eleonora (Nori)*
*Hayes in Milan, Italy, in 1946.*

# *Erwin and Eleonora*
## HAYES

Erwin H. Hayes, known as Hal, met his future wife, Eleonora, in Milan, Italy, at the end of World War II. He had joined the army as a private in 1941 and was subsequently promoted to technical sergeant of the 751st GHQ tank battalion. His regiment began fighting in Tunisia and went on to take part in the campaigns of Naples to Foggia; Anzio, Rome, to the Arno, the North Appenines, and the Po Valley. In June 1944, Hal was commissioned a second lieutenant.

In recognition of the highly effective actions of Hal's battalion during the lengthy Italian campaign, they were given the honor of overseeing the beautiful city of Milan as it returned to normalcy. The battalion commander became, in effect, the mayor of Milan. A leader of the OSS gave a party for the officers of the 751st, which Eleonora Pozzi was invited to attend.

"I had recently received a battlefield promotion to first lieutenant," Hal says. "I spotted this lovely lady the minute she stepped off the elevator and onto the patio where the party was being held. I said to a friend, 'That I have to meet.' He laughed and said, 'Forget it. She's been escorting the colonel around town ever since we arrived.' I told him, 'The colonel's married. I'm going to dance with her.'"

And so he did. Nori, as her friends called her, turned out to be not only beautiful but also an exceptionally brave and accomplished young woman. She came from a prominent Milan family; her parents had built a prosperous construction and engineering firm, and her father was a colonel in the

Italian army. When her father refused to cooperate after Italy joined forces
with Hitler, the Germans sent him to a concentration camp, where he was
treated somewhat better as a senior officer than the other prisoners but witnessed brutal punishments. With Nori's father gone, the full responsibility
of running the family business had fallen to her and her mother.

Hal and Nori fell in love almost at first sight. But the same battlefield
valor and courage that had made it possible for Hal to approach the beautiful Nori and ask her to dance proved an obstacle to their marriage. He
had served a total of 581 days in combat, a long time for a soldier. The
army, presuming they were doing him a favor, decided it was time to ship
the good soldier home to America. Hal, who considered this terrible
news, requested reassignment in an attempt to stay in Italy long enough
to get married—but to no avail.

It would take Hal a year to the day to return to Italy. First he had to
fight with the State Department to get a passport. They told him, with
no trace of irony, "There has been a war over there, and passports are not
being issued for tourists." Hal finally convinced the State Department
that, given his own part in freeing Italy, the least they could do was permit him to go back and marry the woman he loved.

But many hurdles still lay in his path. To get back into Italy, Hal had
to have an Italian visa. The nearest Italian consulate to Spokane, Washington, where his family lived, was all the way in San Francisco, and Hal
had no way to get there. He embarked on another battle by correspondence before he was finally granted a visa.

At last, Hal had his papers but no means of transportation to Italy.
Only one line, the American Export Line headquartered in New York,
was shipping into Italy at the time. Hal contacted the same friend he had
been with in Milan the day he met Nori. That friend happened to live on
Long Island, and he sent Hal the shipping company's address. American
Export Line wrote Hal a vague letter telling him that they did "periodic
sailings," but either there was no specific schedule or they were unwilling
to provide it.

So Hal "took the bull by the horns." He packed a bag and hopped on
the next train to New York. Arriving there on a Saturday morning, he
went directly to the shipping line's offices. A sign on the door said they
were closed on Saturday, but the door was open, so he walked right in.

Two clerks sat in a room containing about thirty empty desks. Hal approached the nearest clerk and quickly explained his situation. "The clerk reluctantly checked in a filing cabinet and, after a brief search, informed me that my file apparently had been shipped to the Seattle office. I told him that I had never been told there was a Seattle office, which was why I was not in Seattle but in New York, and that I was going to be on the next ship sailing for Italy no matter what."

The clerk asked Hal to wait a few minutes while he made a telephone call. "While talking on the phone, he placed his hand over the mouthpiece and asked if I could be ready to sail on the coming Thursday. I said I was ready to sail right then. The clerk talked to the party on the phone for another couple of minutes and hung up. He asked to see my passport and visa, and then he crossed out a name on the list he was working on and entered my name in its place. He told me I was lucky, because he was typing the manifest for the Thursday departure, and once it was finished, it couldn't be changed." Finally, a small stroke of fate had intervened on behalf of Hal and Nori.

When Hal's ship arrived in Genoa, Nori and her family were there to greet him. After a joyous reunion, the couple began the difficult process of obtaining a marriage license and getting permission to be married in a Catholic church. Hal converted to Catholicism, and at long last, they were married on September 28, 1946, in Milan.

They had decided to live in the United States but could not return without encountering a whole new set of bureaucratic difficulties. Nori needed a new passport, and a shipping and air strike had begun. When shipping at last resumed, Nori was a high-priority passenger as the wife of an American serviceman. But Hal himself now had no priority whatsoever. He was considered a mere tourist. Only after many frustrating visits to the American consulate was Hal finally able to return home to the United States with his new wife.

Hal Hayes fought two very different kinds of Italian campaigns. One he fought on the battlefield as a member of the 751st Tank Battalion; the other he fought on paper with bureaucrats on two continents. It was all worth it in the end, though, and Hal considers both campaigns victorious. "After fifty-four wonderful years," Hal says, "Nori and I are still having fun."

*Hal in June 1944, just after being promoted to second lieutenant.*

*Hal being awarded the Silver Star medal by Lieutenant General Mark Clark in August 1944.*

*Telegram sent by Nori to Hal's sister in Seattle, asking for word of Hal because she hadn't heard from him for so long.*

WESTERN UNION

TD41

T.CDU587 INTL=CD MILANO VIA RCA 18 5 11156 DEC 5 PM 3 55

MAURINE OKICICH=

4917 FINDLAY SEATTLE (WASH)=

WORRIED HAVING NOT HEARD FROM HAROLD LET ME KNOW SOMETHING

LOVINGLY=

NORI POZZI.

*Hal and Nori after their wedding in September 1946.*

*Hal and Nori in 1999.*

B ACK ON THE HOME FRONT,
*American women who married or fell
in love with men who immigrated from
overseas and were not U.S. citizens could find their
lives utterly disrupted. Some women married men
before the war who were now regarded as threats
because they retained their German or Italian citizenship. Those countries were among our enemies,
and the American government had to be convinced
that men who retained their citizenship were not
spies or even saboteurs. While their backgrounds were
checked, these men were often separated from their
wives, held in detention camps in several states.
Their experiences characterize a different kind of
World War II love story.*

*Henry and Jane Schlosser in January 1941, before they were married on a ski trip to the Bear Mountain resort in upstate New York, with the Bear Mountain Inn in the background.*

# Henry and Jane
## SCHLOSSER

In 1939, Jane Keller graduated from the Pratt Institute, the well-known art and design college in Brooklyn. Soon after, she found a job at an advertising firm on Fifty-third Street in Manhattan.

One morning in 1940, between Christmas and New Year's Day, she spotted a man in the lobby of her office building. He was dressed jauntily, sporting a hat with a large brim and a European-style double-breasted overcoat. Just as she looked at him, he put a handkerchief to his nose and blew with a loud honk. Jane turned away.

She soon discovered the man was a freelance artist, hired by her agency to work for a few days on a special project. His name was Henry Schlosser. It turned out that he had noticed her in the lobby that day, too. They exchanged pleasantries over the next few days, and on January 3, when they happened to lunch at the same restaurant, he suggested she sit with him.

That lunch launched a lifetime together.

They turned out to have a great deal in common, and conversation flowed with an ease and verve that is usually the hallmark of people who have known each other a very long time.

Henry was German by birth. He first came to the United States in 1928 when he was twenty-three. He loved America and everything about it, from baseball to apple pie. He had brought his German bride to Rochester, New York, where they had two daughters, Marion and Sylvia.

In 1937 the advertising company McCann-Erikson, for which Henry worked for a long time, sent him to Germany to head their offices there. But he disliked Hitler's Germany and wanted to return to America. His wife, however, did not, and they soon divorced. Henry had a very difficult time persuading the German authorities to permit him to leave the country in 1938, but he finally convinced them that with an American salary, he would be in a better position to support his two children. Once he got back to America, he decided to freelance rather than work for a single company, and he settled in New York City.

Jane Keller was born and raised in the Midwest, and her parents were quite conservative. "Henry was not exactly what they had in mind for me," Jane says. "A divorced foreigner with two children who was thirteen years older than I was, an artist—and a freelancer on top of that." But Jane was deeply smitten with Henry and, despite all objections, said yes when he asked her to marry him.

They got a license, but she kept putting off their wedding date, in part because of her parents' disapproval and in part because, as Jane admits, she is given to second thoughts. They eventually had to get another license. The day before the second one expired, September 21, 1941, they finally got married. Despite their hesitations, Jane's parents did attend. Her mother had worked all night to finish Jane's dress.

Henry lived in a sublet at the time, and they decided to find a new place immediately, ending up in the heart of Greenwich Village in an apartment on Bank Street, across from the New School for Social Research. Jane kept her job in advertising and Henry did quite well as a freelancer, often called on by major corporations like RCA and DuPont.

The days went by, and they were very happy. But on March 31, 1942, their doorbell rang. When they answered, two FBI agents confronted them. Henry had never officially become an American citizen. Back in the 1930s, he had started the application process but was interrupted when McCann-Erikson sent him back to Germany. Because of the difficulties he encountered in getting out of Germany, he spent so long abroad that he was required to start the naturalization process all over again, and he just hadn't quite got around to it.

With America at war with Germany and Italy, as well as Japan, the government professed concern regarding the loyalty of people from those countries who were living in America. Today, most know the stories of the internment camps for Japanese-Americans. Fewer know that there were also detention camps for Germans and Italians. Like many artists, Henry had a habit of saving photos and clippings of all sorts that interested him, so his apartment was full of "evidence" that could easily be taken the wrong way by a suspicious officer.

To Jane's horror, Henry was put into detention on Ellis Island in New York Harbor. He had some very distinguished company, including the great Metropolitan Opera star Ezio Pinza, who would later captivate all of America singing "Some Enchanted Evening" when he costarred with Mary Martin in *South Pacific* on Broadway. Pinza was still an Italian citizen, although he had lived in America for many years.

Henry, Pinza, and their fellow detainees were not treated badly. In between writing letters trying to regain his freedom, Henry entertained himself by making water color paintings of the camp. Soon the guards and other Ellis Island officials were offering him what amounted to cigarette money in exchange for a sketch. In the weeks leading up to Christmas, Henry hand-painted wooden toys for family and friends. No matter how well he was treated, though, the fact remained that he was incarcerated, separated from Jane and his livelihood as a commercial artist.

Thanks to his international fame and connections, Pinza was released fairly soon. But things got worse for Henry. He was transferred to Fort Meade in Maryland, and Jane moved to Baltimore and took a job there so that she could see him—for only twenty minutes every two weeks. After three months at Fort Meade, Henry was sent to yet another detention camp in Tennessee. Jane couldn't very well pull up stakes again, so she remained in Baltimore.

She planned to go home to her parents for Christmas of 1942. (Jane does give her parents great credit for never once saying "I told you so" when Henry was taken into custody.) Two days before she was to leave for Roslyn, she got a call from Henry. The letters he wrote from jail to friends and employers who could vouch for him had finally paid off. After a thorough investigation, the government had cleared his name. He didn't know exactly when he would be released, but he assured Jane that everything was all right and he would certainly see her soon. It was the best Christmas present Jane could have asked for.

*Henry on their
ski trip to Bear
Mountain.*

*Henry and Jane on
their wedding day,
September 21, 1941.*

*A marriage certificate Henry painted and lettered for their first anniversary, while he was interned at Fort Meade.*

*A painting Henry did for Jane's birthday
while at Fort Meade.*

*A newspaper article about an exhibition of toys sent by German children to America in thanks for donations to a school feeding program.*

The Philadelphia Inquirer

a d    FRIDAY, FEBRUARY 14, 1947    22

### GIFTS FROM GERMAN CHILDREN

School children of Darmstadt, Germany, grateful for gifts that made possible a school feeding program, made 1000 toys for American children, and sent them to the American Friends Service Committee. Henry Schlosser, Mrs. Jane Schlosser (left) and Miss Miriam Beck arrange the toys for exhibitions in schools.

They were finally reunited on January 6, 1943, and settled down again in New York. When their daughter, Heidi, was born in November of 1943, they decided to give up their work in advertising and moved to a farm near Roslyn, New York. Henry applied again for citizenship as soon as his detention was over, and in 1945 he at last became an American citizen. There, sparked by the enjoyment Henry had found making toys as Christmas presents, they started a business designing and making wooden toys. Since materials were still scarce due to the war, they used scrap material from bomb cases. The toys were sold nationwide as "Bonnie Barn" toys. Later in 1945, their son, Jon, was born, and the farm they were renting was sold, so they had to move again.

This time they moved to Chester County, near Jane's parents' new home. Henry and Jane ran a toy-importing business in the 1950s and '60s for shops called Christmas Stocking and Bonnie Barn, which they opened in various towns in Pennsylvania and in Ocean City, New Jersey. By 1973 they decided to sell the last shop they kept open, in King of Prussia, Pennsylvania, and started collecting and selling antique toys, establishing themselves as premier American dealers.

"We had fifty lovely years together," Jane remembers. "Henry died before we reached our actual fiftieth anniversary, but we made it to the anniversary of our first lunch together." Jane herself now runs a shop in the "antique country" around Adamstown, Pennsylvania. It is overflowing with exquisite treasures originally made for children but now coveted by adult collectors. Seeing the fanciful antiques every day reminds her of the wonderful life she and Henry shared.

WHILE THE UNRULY AMERICAN *west might have come as a shock to war brides from overseas, the rustic setting sometimes offered unexpected amenities to new brides and officers during the war—if you knew where to look. Many young couples did everything they could to be together for as long as possible before the husband was shipped overseas. Army air force pilots had to train over a longer period of time than those serving in the ground forces. Many of their wives, through pure ingenuity and tenacity, found ways to be with them during these long months of training. In makeshift and money-short accommodations, wives remained determined to make the best of their situation. Occasionally, a young couple even got lucky and stumbled into unusual circumstances that they would remember with great fondness for the rest of their lives.*

# *Wharton and Miriam*

## SCHNEIDER

When Morton Schneider got his first driver's license at the age of sixteen, someone at the DMV made a mistake and issued the license in the name of Wharton. Mr. Schneider liked his dignified new name well enough, so he decided not to fight city hall.

A few years later, when he sought a commission in the army air force during World War II, he realized problems might arise from the inconsistency. The army would want a transcript of his high school records, which carried his birth name of Morton. Surprisingly, the army took his situation right in stride; they told him they would add the name Morton to his file as an alias and request his high school records accordingly. He served as an army air force pilot officially named Wharton Schneider, and he's carried the name ever since.

Wharton met his Brooklyn-born wife, Miriam, while stationed in California in 1943. She was visiting an aunt in Hollywood when they happened to run into each other. They quickly realized they were meant for each other and got married in Hollywood that very December.

Shortly after the wedding, Wharton was transferred to Fort Sumner in New Mexico. The army informed him they had no available accommodations for spouses, but he and Miriam decided to give it a try anyway. Surely they could find someplace for her to live. The base turned out to be in the middle of nowhere, and Miriam ended up in a rundown hotel in Clovis, New Mexico, sixty miles east of her husband—hardly the best situation for a young woman.

A few weeks after their move to New Mexico, Wharton went out to dinner in the small town of Santa Rosa, New Mexico, fifty miles west of the base, with a couple of fellow pilots. When they finished eating, he went into a back room to telephone Miriam. They spoke on the phone for a long time, and when Wharton returned to the front of the bar, he realized that not a soul was left in the place. What was more, he was locked in.

Wharton immediately ran back to the phone, called the local operator, and apprised her of his situation. She asked his location, but he wasn't even sure where he was. The operator instructed him to go to the window, look out, and then come back and tell her what he saw. So Wharton walked over to the window, peered outside, and described it to the operator, who assured him that she'd call the owner, who would hopefully let him out. She soon called back to tell Wharton that the owner, Mr. Medley, was in the shower and wouldn't be able to get there for another fifteen minutes; in the meantime, Wharton should feel free to help himself to a cigar or some cream pie. More concerned with getting out than having cream pie, Wharton decided not to take advantage of the owner's kind offer. Luckily, he didn't have to wait too long.

When the owner showed up, he and Wharton hit it off immediately. Wharton learned during their friendly banter that Mr. Medley and his brother owned half the businesses in Santa Rosa: the restaurant, the movie theater and the drugstore. He also knew of a small motor inn with cooking facilities—perfect for Miriam.

Miriam moved there in the blink of an eye. It was nothing fancy, but at least she could cook for herself and for Wharton when he was off duty. Mr. Medley even drove the 110 miles to Clovis to help Miriam move to Santa Rosa. According to Wharton, the Medley brothers couldn't have been nicer to a young pilot and his wife—now pregnant—if they'd all been friends since childhood. One brother headed the local rationing board, so Wharton and Miriam got all the gas they needed. And one night, due to the distance Wharton still had to travel from Fort Sumner, he and Miriam arrived at the movie theater ten minutes after the feature had begun. The Medley brother in charge stopped the film, rewound it, and started it again from the beginning, just for them.

All over the country, the wives of young servicemen made do under difficult circumstances, having a hard time making ends meet. But one young couple in Santa Rosa, New Mexico, had a very nice time of it, thanks to two brothers named Medley.

Miriam was due to give birth about a week before Wharton was scheduled to go overseas. Suddenly, though, Wharton was asked to fly a special mission a few days earlier than originally planned. He asked if he could please stick around, since his first child was coming any day. The army relented and granted Wharton special permission to stay, transferring him to Kingman Army Air Force Base, outside of Kingman, Arizona.

According to a lot of soldiers, the army was usually pretty good about that sort of thing, although a lot depended on the attitude of one's superior officers. Wharton turned out to be luckier than he could have imagined. The plane he had been asked to fly on the special mission crashed, killing both pilots. That kind of eerie luck befell many soldiers during the war. But rather than feeling like they'd been saved by a miracle, those who survived just quietly accepted their good fortune. They knew all too well that next time around, things might not work out so much in their favor.

Miriam soon gave birth to a daughter at the base hospital. Shortly after the birth, Wharton had to say good-bye when Miriam's mother arrived to accompany Miriam and the baby back east for the duration of the war.

The air force sent Wharton to India to fly supplies over the Hump—the name pilots gave to the treacherous route over the Himalayas—and deliver them to General Chiang Kai-shek's forces in China: "the forgotten war," Wharton calls it, as his role in World War II doesn't get much press. But while the public may have forgotten, military historians know that the air force sent only the very best pilots to India to fly the Hump. The Himalayas rose dauntingly high, the weather was subject to wild fluctuations, and if your plane went down, you had virtually no chance of rescue. In order to survive the treacherous flight conditions, you not only had to possess an extraordinary instinct for flying, you had to have nerves of steel. Wharton is too modest a fellow to admit any of this, but to those who know, the mere mention of having flown the Hump speaks volumes.

After the hostilities in India diminished somewhat, Wharton was assigned for a few months as a flying safety officer in Calcutta. He received one last assignment to fly General Stone from Shanghai back to

WAR DEPARTMENT
HEADQUARTERS OF THE ARMY AIR FORCES
WASHINGTON

March 6, 1943

PERSONNEL ORDERS )
NO.   56        )

EXTRACT

4.  Pursuant to authority contained in paragraph 2, sub-paragraph 2, Army Regulations 35-1480, dated October 10, 1942, the following-named officers, Air Corps (AUS), each of whom holds an aeronautical rating, are hereby required to participate in regular and frequent aerial flights, at such times as they are called to active duty with the Army Air Forces, U. S. Army, under competent authority, and are authorized to participate in regular and frequent aerial flights while on an inactive status, in accordance with the provisions of paragraph 52, A.R. 95-15, dated April 21, 1930.

> 1st Lt. William Whitney Ward, (O-514738)
> 2nd Lt. Marshall Charles Benedict, (O-514641)
> 2nd Lt. Charles Castleman Bulger, (O-514746)
> 2nd Lt. Manford Milton Owen, Jr., (O-514625)
> 2nd Lt. Wharton Leo Schneider, (O-514626)

All orders in conflict with this order are revoked.

By command of Lieutenant General Arnold:

J. M. Bevans,
Colonel, Air Corps,
Director of Personnel.

OFFICIAL:

OFFICIAL

John H. Walls,
Captain, Air Corps,
Assistant Chief,
Military Personnel Division.

Note:  When attached to pay voucher for purpose of collecting flying pay this order or true copies thereof, should be in duplicate and accompanied by duplicate –
(a)  Copies of order calling the officer to active duty.
(b)  Flight certificate of officer, duly signed by the Commanding Officer as called for by existing regulations.

3-7208-2, AF

*Wharton Schneider's commission as a second lieutenant.*

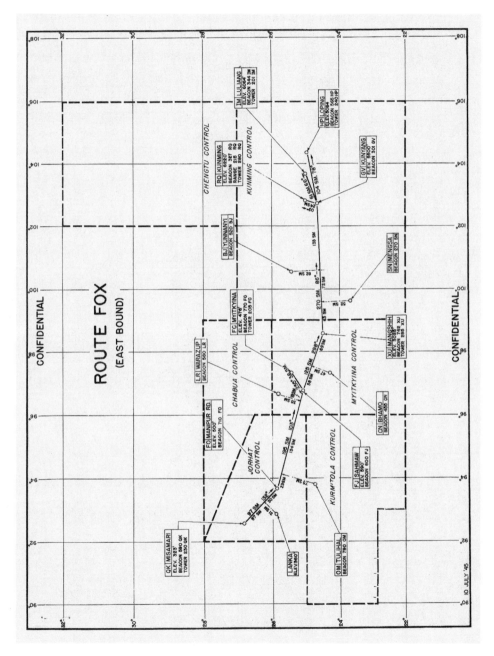

*The flight route over "the Hump," the treacherous Himalayas.*

the United States. The day before Christmas, 1945, he arrived home to be with his wife and daughter.

At the reunions of pilots who flew the Hump, Wharton and his fellow Hump veterans no doubt regale one another with tales and memories of those harrowing days trying to judge what the crazy winds of the Himalayas might do next. But in his day-to-day life, he prefers to talk about the happy days he spent with his young wife in Santa Rosa, New Mexico, under the ever helpful gaze of the Medley brothers.

SIXTEEN MILLION AMERICAN MEN *and women served in uniform in one branch of the service or another during World War II. Almost two-thirds of them were in the army, including the army air force. Four million served in the navy. Only a few more than five hundred thousand served in the marines who fought some of the toughest battles of the war in the South Pacific. Then there was the even smaller cadre of men who served in the merchant marine, who got supplies from the United States to Allied ports around the world. They faced grave danger throughout the war, even though the men didn't serve in any branch of the service. No supply was more important than the oil transported by the Esso fleet.*

*Harry and Mary Lou Heffelfinger aboard*
*one of Harry's ships.*

# *Harry E. and Mary Lou*
# HEFFELFINGER

---

While the stories of the men and women who served in the armed forces during World War II are featured most prominently in this book, there were other individuals who faced the dangers of military service even though they were not in the army, the navy, or the marines. One such man was Harry E. Heffelfinger, a captain in the fleet of Standard Oil tankers that delivered vital fuel to the Allied countries throughout the war, despite grave danger.

The crews on oil tankers were accustomed to being away from their loved ones for considerable periods of time, but the war required even longer tours of duty, as well as the constant threat of attack. These crews were every bit as crucial in the battle for freedom as military personnel. Most of their time was spent doing the same hard work they'd always done, but the everyday perils of sailing the high seas with an inflammable cargo were considerably intensified by the knowledge that they could fall under fire at any time from any direction by enemy ships or subs.

Harry Heffelfinger was born in landlocked Indiana in the first year of the twentieth century. Although he spent much of his youth wishing he could own a small farm, instead he went to sea. He shipped out for the first time in 1918, working on U.S. Shipping Board vessels. In December 1921, he joined the Esso fleet, aboard the *W. J. Hannah*. He worked his way up to master by July of 1933, and he served as the captain of many ships over the next two decades in the marine division of Humble Oil & Refining Company, a major Standard Oil constituent.

In 1940 he began dating Mary Lou Harris, a registered pediatric nurse in Newark, New Jersey, whom he had met through a mutual friend. They soon became engaged. Writing from aboard the *Peter Hurll* in September 1940, en route to Rio de Janeiro, Harry declared, "I'm having a terrible time snapping out of this tropical lethargy, what with a full moon, millions of stars, and you to dream of. Can you wonder I'm in a trance? . . . You have me right up in the clouds and I love it, and you, and life, and that makes the sun shine night and day for me."

In an even more ardent letter, Harry told Mary Lou that he knew it was raining in Newark, where she was, but added, "If we were there together it would be in full bloom, rain or shine. It's always that way with you, darling Mary Lou, your radiant beauty, and I want to come home to bask in it, naked too, must have the full benefit of your radiance. Baby, can I swing on the ice-box door?"

Harry sent Mary Lou bottles of perfume that he bought in his travels around the Caribbean and South America, when the ship put in at ports from Aruba to Venezuela to Brazil, scents like Shocking, Belladagia, and Scandal. Mary Lou always dabbed some on her letters back to Harry.

Though the war was already raging in Europe, the U.S. had not entered, and American shipping was not yet at danger from the German U-boat threat. Harry's letters from this period describe the usual daily life aboard ship, remarking on the few passengers, or lamenting the fact that stores of fresh food picked up along the way had been ruined by the ship's terrible new cook. Matters certainly improved in the food department on a subsequent voyage. With the kind of flourish usually reserved for luxury liners, a typed menu "tendered to" six named passengers with "The Compliments of Captain H. E. Heffelfinger" on December 18, 1940, included hearts of celery and salted almonds, cream of tomato soup, both roast turkey and Virginia ham, four vegetables, fresh salad, ice cream, fruit, and "Surprise Cake." Indeed, on board an American commercial ship in 1940, the war in Europe might well seem not to be happening at all. But as the captain of an oil tanker, Harry knew a good deal about what German subs were doing to British shipping, and the day would soon come when his letters would ominously portray the coming threat.

The day before the sumptuous feast Harry invited his passengers to, President Roosevelt discussed for the first time with members of his cabinet his idea for the Lend-Lease program, which would allow the beleaguered British to purchase food and raw materials, weapons, vehicles and other products from the United States without payment. The bill proposing the program was put before the still-isolationist Congress in January 1941 and passed with the crucial support of the Republican secretary of war, Henry L. Stimson, in March of that year. The Lend-Lease program was one of the most generous acts of assistance ever undertaken by one country on behalf of another.

The same month the Lend-Lease bill went to Congress, Harry and Mary Lou were married in Newark, New Jersey. After Harry returned to his ship, his letters from those subsequent trips are filled with testament to the fact that American commercial ships were no long safe in international waters. Harry wrote from Aruba: "Just got the lowdown on what happened to Capt. Bloomquist, it's rather a long story. Those dirty Germans, they torpedoed him without warning, put three torpedoes into the ship. Lucky everyone on board wasn't killed."

In another letter he told Mary Lou that one of the *Peter Hurll*'s sister tankers, returning from the Azores, had encountered a lifeboat adrift in the Atlantic. There were twelve men in it, all dead, apparently from starvation and thirst. The heavy clothes the dead sailors were wearing indicated that their ship must have been attacked somewhere in the North Atlantic and that they had drifted south, possibly for weeks.

By the end of that year, America had plunged into the war, and Mary Lou worried that her husband would be drafted. Harry wrote to her, "Don't worry about the draft board. Hell, the Army would be easy in comparison to this job." Besides, Harry was far too valuable where he was, transporting critical oil supplies.

Oil for the war effort was in such tight supply that strict gas rationing was instituted on the home front. By the fall of 1942, only three gallons of gas were allowed per week for American family cars, although doctors were allowed more, especially in rural areas with few hospitals where house calls were essential.

After the United States entered the war, the Atlantic routes plied by the tankers in the Standard Oil fleet became highly treacherous. By the end of January 1942, eleven German U-boats began stealthy operations along the East Coast of the United States, and their number quickly increased into the twenties. Their targets were usually merchant ships, and the bodies of sailors began washing up on the beaches of Florida.

The greatest danger to American ships came in the first few months after the U.S. entered the war. The British navy was furious with the U.S. Navy high command during this time; British merchant ships were being sunk, too, and the American navy refused to listen to British advice, despite the fact that the British had been dealing with U-boats for eighteen months. After the war, Winston Churchill declared that the only thing that truly frightened him during the war was the U-boat situation. He was greatly relieved when the U.S. Navy came to understand the peril involved and how to deal with it.

The public was not informed in any detail about these developments. Military censorship controlled not only what was published in newspapers and broadcast over the radio but also what could be written home to loved ones.

The crews aboard Esso ships technically came under the same censorship rules as members of the armed services, but the enforcement was not as strict, and in a letter sent from Aruba on May 2, 1942, Harry told Mary Lou a story that horrified her:

> Since you are curious to know if I had any excitement coming down, yes, we did. Don't know how much the censor will pass, but if you are anxious, we encountered the Nazis hand-to-hand, so to speak. He had me in a tight spot for a while, but we drove him off with the machine guns, nobody hurt on this side but I hope we gave him a belly full. It happened at night when we couldn't see the results. Two nights previous to that a sub opened up on two ships just ahead of me, close, yet far enough for me to see all the action but not be involved. Things were plenty hot up that way. We sailors are going to have a score to settle with those crazy Nazis even after this war is over. Gallant men they are, they sneak alongside of a ship at night and let go with everything they have.

Harry later told the story in more detail for a book published in 1946 by Standard Oil about the 135 vessels of the Esso fleet that transported 665 million barrels of oil during the war. Noting that armament had just been installed on the *Peter Hurll,* Harry relates how his ship and two others moved out of Hampton Roads, Virginia. The lead ship was the *Mercury Sun,* with the *Gulf of Mexico* second, followed by the *Peter Hurll.* On the first night out of Hampton Roads, Harry saw tracer bullets in the darkness ahead—the *Gulf of Mexico* was under machine-gun fire from a U-boat. Harry changed course immediately, and his ship escaped in the darkness. The other two vessels also survived that encounter, but the *Mercury Sun* was sunk six weeks later in the Caribbean.

More serious problems for the *Peter Hurll* developed the following night. "About 10 o'clock," Harry recalled in 1946,

> Chief Engineer Elliot C. Daniels called the bridge and said he would have to stop the port engine to make repairs. We were able to make only about seven knots on one engine. I called out the gun crew. It was a fine clear night and we were only about a mile and a half off shore. A submarine surfaced about 300 to 400 yards away and began firing machine guns at us, the tracer bullets coming close over the wheelhouse. We fired back with our 50 calibers on the bridge. I decided to try to ram the U-boat. When we headed for her she crash-dived. I phoned the engine room and called for all the revolutions we could get. We ran full speed on our starboard engine for about two and half hours and never saw the submarine again.

Harry speculated that the U-boat must have been running low on torpedoes and did not want to waste one on a ship headed south and loaded with ballast, not oil.

A letter Harry wrote to Mary Lou about this encounter was mailed from Curacao in June 1942. It was marked as having been read by a censor. Words were not blacked out, as usual, but actually cut out of the letter with a razor blade. Missing, for example, was a reference to how long the voyage down had taken, as well as a reference to another ship. But the censor did not remove these two frightening sentences: "The damn Nazis broadcast from Berlin that they had sunk us. So I guess they have us on their list." The U-boat portrayed its run-in with the *Peter Hurll* as a triumph. Distortions of casualty figures, and false accounts of planes downed and ships sunk, occurred on both sides during World War II, in part because hard numbers were sometimes difficult to ascertain. The Germans, however, were particularly prone to inflate their damage and casualty estimates.

While the U-boat threat along the East Coast and down into the Caribbean periodically abated, Harry and the other captains in the oil fleet never knew when the Nazis would increase the pressure again. Hitler often seemed to value the element of surprise over other military considerations, which had the desired effect of keeping the Allies continually on edge, although his orders sometimes went against the advice of his own officers and, in the end, undermined the German military.

Years later, Mary Lou told her children that she spent the war years dreading an overseas call to tell her that Harry's ship had been attacked and that he had been wounded or killed. As for Harry, he spent a good deal of his free time writing letters to her that continually asked for news of home. Harry and Mary Lou's first child, their son, Phil (who was nick-named Skipper), was born November 1, 1942, and Harry constantly inquired about how his son was coming along and whether the family's rambunctious dog, Smokey, was behaving himself. One such query was answered by Mary Lou in a brief Western Union cablegram sent to Harry at the Royal British Hotel, Glasgow, Scotland. It read,

FAMILY UNDER CONTROL BUT LONELY STAY WELL LOVE

Only a few of Mary Lou's letters to Harry have survived, but they are lively and full of amusing stories. On December 22, 1943, she wrote a letter that began, "I'm very lonesome for you but that is an old story—yes, no? Nonetheless, what you'd have on your hands if you were home!!!" After telling him about the muddled marriage plans of a relative, she turned to her efforts to decorate the house. "Got down last year's ornaments & such—even the stand & it begins to feel Xmasy—hung bells & pine cones on the front door—they tinkle & Smokey is quite overcome—when he breaks down the door getting in he has a joyous time barking at 'em—all I do is just go & pick up the pieces. Four times I've pinned 'em back on the door (so far)." Her report on baby Phil reflected the vicissitudes of new motherhood: "Phil continues to be the Tarzan of 10 Jerome Street—now it's temper, so much so that Mrs. K. rushed upstairs to see if he was hurt. . . . Told her I was letting him cool off—so she proceeded to pick him up & love him back to sweetness. Hmm, did I ever feel the fool."

In another letter, Mary Lou commented on the public's failure to fully appreciate the importance and danger of the work that civilians like Harry and his crew members were doing, and that they made just as valuable a contribution as those in navy uniform. "If only they'd . . . realize how wonderful you people are. You go out in this weather and take a physical beating plus the horror that is constantly lurking in the sea— then you come ashore and are quiet about your discomforts—but some of these punks dash around in a uniform and have people kissing their feet. 'Taint fair, dear & you know it."

But there was one compensating advantage to Harry's civilian status: He did get home to see Mary Lou more often than most members of the armed services. These respites might have been short, occurring only once every several months, but they meant a great deal to both Harry and Mary Lou. One such visit home resulted in Mary Lou becoming pregnant again, and she gave birth to their daughter, Mary Jane, nicknamed Missi, on April 8, 1944.

Two months after Missi was born, the D-Day invasion took place, and from then on, Mary Lou worried less about her husband. The German military concentrated on efforts to stave off the Allied forces fighting their way toward Berlin, and the U-boats, having lost the French ports they used as bases, ceased to be a threat.

After the war, Harry continued to serve as the captain of numerous ships in the Standard Oil fleet. In 1952 he became group captain, and in November 1959 he was made assistant port captain, a position he held until his retirement in 1963, after more than forty-one years with the company. He died a year later, a much honored man who had traded in his early dreams of owning a small farm in Indiana to spend his life at sea.

Mary Lou Heffelfinger suffered a stroke in 1965, a year after her husband's death, and subsequently moved into a nursing home. She was allowed to bring only one suitcase of personal belongings aside from clothes. After her death in 1973, a good friend took charge of the suitcase for safekeeping. In the winter of 2000, the friend rediscovered the suitcase stored away in the attic, and asked Harry and Mary Lou's daughter, Missi, if she wanted it. Missi recalls that her heart leaped when she heard the suitcase existed. There was just one thing she hoped would be in it. When Missi was about sixteen, she came across something fascinating in the hall linen closet at the top of the stairs. It was a pink tin box that had once contained three pounds of Louis Sherry chocolates. In the box were several packets of old letters, tissue-thin and handwritten, tied with purple ribbons. Quickly realizing that they were written by her father to her mother during the war, she started to read them. But before long, her mother came upstairs, saw what she was up to, told her sternly that those letters were private, and took them away.

Sure enough, there was that same pink tin in the suitcase, just as Missi had hoped. Just a few days after recovering the letters, Missi's brother told her that he had seen a notice in the newspaper requesting World War II love stories for this book. The timing struck Missi as more than mere coincidence, and even though her mother had considered the letters too private for Missi to read when she was a teenager, Missi and her brother both felt that the letters honored their parents and that their story of the war should be shared with others. After all, those letters had been carefully preserved a very long time because they were so special.

FORM NO. 6.

# WESTERN UNION
## (THE WESTERN UNION TELEGRAPH COMPANY)
### (INCORPORATED IN THE STATE OF NEW YORK, U.S.A., WITH LIMITED LIABILITY.)

# CABLEGRAM
ANGLO-AMERICAN TELEGRAPH CO., LD.                    CANADIAN NATIONAL TELEGRAPHS.

RECEIVED AT 8, WATERLOO STREET, GLASGOW, C.2. (Tel. No. Central. 6363.)
Kirkintilloch, 1782.  (After office hours.)

2 NEWARKNJ 19 12 1207P                    1943 MAR 13  AM 7  15


CAPT HARRY HEFFELFINGER CARE MARSH

ROYAL BRITISH HOTEL GLASGOW


FAMILY UNDER CONTROL BUT LONELY STAY WELL LOVE

    MARY HEFFLEFINGER +

*The Western Union cablegram Mary Lou sent to Harry when he was in
Glasglow, Scotland.*

*Harry and Mary Lou
at a black-tie dance.*

EVEN IN THE MIDST OF WAR, *humor somehow survives. In fact, humor may be one of the key things that got the soldiers through the fear and pain of being at the front during World War II. The humorous banter in which the soldiers sometimes engaged was often rough, cynical, even dark, a fragile moment of laughter in the horror. As they look back on their experience, many of those who fought in World War II—and the women they loved—can muster a wry comment here and there about it. But genuinely funny stories, the kind that engender cozy, happy, warm laughter, emerge only rarely during wartime.*

*Al Goldis at flight school in 1943.*

# Alfred and Shirley

## GOLDIS

Al Goldis was a twenty-year-old sophomore at the prestigious Massachusetts Institute of Technology in the spring of 1940. On the last day of March of that year, he showed up at a "sweet sixteen" party in Newton, a dozen miles away. He hadn't officially been invited, but the brother of the birthday girl, who also attended MIT, had invited a classmate, who in turn had suggested that Al tag along. Little did he know what that suggestion might lead to.

Shirley Shapiro, in whose honor the party was being given, was perfectly happy to have her big brother's college friends there. Al spent a few moments talking with her, but he, along with most of the other young men at the party, was mesmerized by one of Shirley's friends, a tall, leggy blonde. She was a drum majorette, which every girl wanted to be, and boys were attracted to her, Al recalls, "like bees to the honeypot."

Some weeks later, Al was invited to a big Intra-Fraternity Council (IFC) dance weekend. He didn't belong to a fraternity, but these bashes were usually open to anyone who had friends in any of the fraternities involved. Al invited his sister to come up from Brooklyn, where the family lived, for the occasion. He hoped to show her a good time. But she didn't go out much, as she was painfully shy, and at the last minute, she decided not to join him.

Al wasn't having any luck finding another date until the same classmate who had invited him to the party where they'd met Shirley Shapiro suggested that he give her a call. The dance was that very night, April 26, so he called her at school. Students weren't supposed to take personal calls, but Al convinced a woman in the principal's office that it was a real emergency. When Shirley came to the phone, he implored her, "Don't say no right away," then told her about the big party in glowing detail. She said yes.

They had a great time that evening and started to see each other quite regularly after that. In fact, Al recalls that he almost flunked out of school because he spent more time on the phone with Shirley than he did studying.

By June of that year, the two began to talk seriously about marriage, but Al wanted to graduate first and get established, so they agreed to postpone engagement and marriage for about four years. But when Pearl Harbor was bombed in December 1941, they realized they might have to postpone their wedding even longer. Al enlisted in January and went off to learn to fly for the U.S. Army Air Corps.

Al graduated from flying school in February 1943. Corps tradition required that his wings be pinned on by someone "near and dear," so he invited Shirley to come to Blytheville, Arkansas, to do the honors. While she was visiting, they became engaged. Shirley returned to Newton, Massachusetts, and Al headed off first to Tucson, Arizona, to learn to fly B-24s and then to Herrington, Kansas, to pick up a plane and a crew. After a month of further flight training, he shipped out to Benghazi, Cyrenaica (Libya), where he was to report to the Ninth Bomber Command for combat duty.

Al and his crew arrived in Cyrenaica on Sunday, August 1, 1943, just as many crews were returning from a notorious treetop-level bombing mission over the Ploesti oil fields in Romania, held by the Germans. The scene was horrific. Badly damaged B-24s streamed in for precarious landings, and bloodied airmen were being loaded into ambulances.

Al's was the first replacement crew to arrive after the Ninth Bomber Command had been organized. Because the crews who had been there for months already were exhausted, he flew missions every day. At this time in the war, no crew was supposed to fly more than thirty missions, but the military soon increased that number to fifty out of necessity. When Al and his crew hit the fifty mark, the flight surgeon ordered them to go for some R&R.

There weren't many places for tired soldiers to go for R&R then. The surgeon explained to Al that Tel Aviv had been designated by the U.S. Army Air Force as its sole R&R station in the entire North African and Middle Eastern theater because it was the only place to get a clean room, a hot bath, and decent food. So Al and his crew flew to Tel Aviv.

After a couple of days in Tel Aviv, they found themselves on board a Red Cross tour bus, gallivanting around the Levant. One of the stops was Damascus, in Syria, and Al and his crew decided they had to sample a belly-dancing nightclub while they were there. The female Red Cross guides wanted to see some real belly dancing as well—Al hastens to add that belly dancing is not a burlesque attraction in the Middle East but a folk-dance art form—but according to Muslim law, women were not allowed outdoors except for an hour at noon with their children, and certainly not in nightclubs. Al and the other guys decided they'd try to get the women in anyway; Al protested to the manager of the club that American mores were different and should be respected. Surprisingly, the man agreed to let the women in.

The youngest and slimmest belly dancers came on first, but as the show continued, the real stars appeared, each one older and heavier than the last. The superstar was the fattest of all, but she made every inch of flesh ripple with expression, and the place went wild.

After the show, Al persuaded the youngest and slimmest of the dancers—in his eyes the prettiest, even if she was the least accomplished in the Syrian view—to go out with him. To his astonishment, he discovered that "going out" meant getting in a taxi and going to her home, where she rousted her parents from bed and the house so she and Al could take it over. Once their "involvement," as he refers to it, was over, Al decided the most sensible thing to do was head back to his hotel. Wandering through the dark streets that night, with mysterious shadows cast on the whitewashed walls, he says he felt in more danger than he had on any of his combat missions. Not till he got back to his hotel did he realize that he should have been on his guard even earlier; he had been "rolled" by the dancer and didn't have a dime left.

The next afternoon, the Red Cross guides took Al and his crew to a tea at the home of a wealthy British-educated merchant—what Americans would call a "merchant prince." The tea was strong and the crumpets were excellent. The host then showed his guests around his home, which was exquisite and decorated with many precious artifacts. He was clearly a man of great taste, and he charmed them all.

In a large atrium around which the house was built, rimmed by arches, Al noticed that under each arch lay a couch, and on each couch lolled a beautiful woman, "peeling a grape or gorging on a box of chocolates." Al thought to himself that this must be the man's harem, but as it turned out, all eight of them were his wives. In keeping with Muslim culture, they were not introduced to the men.

The merchant invited Al and the others to come to his shop the next day. It was a dazzling place. Particularly impressive was a set of inlaid living room furniture upholstered in royal blue plush velvet that the merchant said was about to be shipped to England. A British captain furnishing a new house for himself and his bride had stopped by and bought it for £8,000—in those days the equivalent of $40,000.

In another room lay bolts of cloth, the likes of which Al had never seen before. Silks and satins and brocades ravished the eye, particularly a silver brocade and a gold brocade, both shot through with threads of real gold and silver. Given the cost of the bedroom set, Al hardly dared to ask the price.

Miraculously, the merchant turned out to be selling the silver brocade for only about $12 a yard, which, the young women of the Red Cross quietly assured Al, was an extraordinary bargain. Such cloth would cost many times more in New York, probably $40 or $50 a yard. Al knew immediately that the silver brocade would make a perfect wedding gown for Shirley, whom he planned to marry as soon as he got home to America. But he had a problem. He sheepishly had to explain to the merchant that he had no money to pay for the brocade, since a belly dancer had picked his pocket the night before.

The merchant waved his hand airily. No problem, he assured Al, taking down a dusty old ledger from a shelf; Al could pay later. In the ledger, the merchant wrote down Al's name, rank, and serial number, and guaranteed him that the seven yards the Red Cross guides had decided would be enough for a dress with a full train would be shipped off to Shirley in Newton.

Al could not imagine by what channels that shipment would take place, but he decided not to inquire too closely. After all, he hadn't paid for it, so if it didn't arrive, well, so what?

Soon Al and his crew were back in the air over North Africa. Base operations had been relocated to Tunis by then, and they had to catch up with their unit. Al flew another twenty missions over North Africa and Italy, earning a Silver Star, a Distinguished Flying Cross, and several other medals. Finally, he was ordered back to America, but he got held up in Dakar in Senegal for two weeks, "a garden spot if ever there were one," as Al recalls, and during that time the D-Day invasion of Normandy took place. He got the word while "lollygagging" on the bean in Dakar.

When he returned to Newton at the end of June 1944, he was pleased to discover that Shirley had actually received the silver brocade and was thrilled with it. Her family persuaded her cousin Ida, who was the best seamstress in the Boston area, to make the wedding dress—she could not resist working with such exquisite fabric.

Al and Shirley were married on July 10, 1944. Shirley looked beautiful beyond words in her silver brocade from Damascus. It was the chief topic of conversation among the hundreds of family members and friends who gathered at the Belmont country club for the reception. Al wore his uniform, as required. He was, after all, still in the army air force, and the war was still on.

Over the next few months, accompanied by Shirley, Al worked as an air/sea rescue instructor first at Chanute Field in Champaign-Urbana, Illinois, and then at March Field in California. When the war in the Pacific ended, Al was the very first man at March Field to be demobilized. He won this distinction based on points accumulated through length of service, number of missions flown, and medals received. He and Shirley, already pregnant with their daughter, returned to Newton to live with her parents while he resumed and completed his studies at MIT.

One day, almost two years after their wedding, the doorbell rang while Al was at school. When Shirley answered the door, a gentleman with a pronounced British accent confronted her. Did a Mr. Alfred Collins live there? he inquired.

"No," Shirley replied. "My husband is Alfred Goldis."

The gentleman politely suggested that perhaps he had the name wrong, as the handwriting on the paper he had was unclear. Did she, by any chance, know anything about several yards of silver brocade?

"Why, yes," said Shirley, quite surprised. "That was used for my wedding dress."

The polite but firm British gentleman turned out to be a bill collector. Al had forgotten to send payment to the merchant prince for the brocade. Shirley went to the bank the next day and converted dollars to British pounds to take care of the debt.

Al maintains that Shirley has told the story of the bill collectors and brocade innumerable times. But being the wonderful wife she is, she has never in their fifty-five years of marriage asked him point-blank how he got rolled in the Damascan Casbah. Of course we know she knows, or this story would not be included here, as it is, with Shirley's full approval.

*Shirley in her wedding dress made from the silver brocade Al sent her, and Al in full uniform.*

*Al and Shirley at home, Christmas 1998.*

O F COURSE, MANY LOVE AFFAIRS
during the war ran into difficulties.

A couple often decided that, despite their mutual affection, they weren't entirely ready to be man and wife—they just got caught up in the excitement of the moment. When the war ended and life returned to normal, they simply chose to go their own ways. Though some might stay in touch for a while, contact was usually lost before long. But then circumstances, sheer curiosity, or a sense of loss might engender a reunion. What might happen if that passion from the war reignited, this time under entirely different circumstances?

*Ron and Marilyn Smith in 1944.*

# *Ron*

# SMITH

---

Ron Smith served as a torpedoman on the submarine U.S.S. *Seal,* one of only a handful of American subs to make it all the way through the war, from 1942 to 1945.

Ron met his first wife during a repair layover in San Francisco in 1944. The crew had divided into two groups, one of which remained with the sub while the other went on leave. When the latter group returned to the sub, those who had stayed went home to loved ones. Ron was in the second group, and since there was little to do aboard the *Seal* while it was being refitted, he had a good deal of time on his hands.

The crew lived in barracks onshore rather than on the sub. On Easter Sunday, he and a shipmate named Joe were the last to leave the barracks. They took the ferry over to the city, had breakfast, and decided to have a beer at a favorite bar on Georgia Street. The bar was closed, of course, on Easter Sunday morning, and Joe, somewhat out of the blue, suggested that maybe they should go to church. Ron agreed that wasn't such a bad idea—they could use a church service after what they'd been through in the Pacific.

They walked back a few blocks to a big church they'd passed earlier, but the service was just letting out. "Well, we had good intentions," Joe declared. Then they noticed two pretty girls coming out of the church, and the focus of their intentions changed instantly.

The two sailors fell into step on either side of the girls. When Ron said a cordial hello to the girl next to him, she retorted, "I don't talk to strangers, especially sailors." But she turned to look at him. He noticed she was even prettier up close, with long, dark brown hair and blue eyes, and a perfect figure. Ron didn't realize he was staring until she repeated that she didn't talk to strangers, but she smiled as she said it.

Ron and Joe introduced themselves and asked the girls' names. The one Ron was interested in said her name was Marilynn, "with two 'N's." Ron pointed out that now they weren't strangers anymore, and Marilynn replied that sailors were all alike.

Presently, the girls stopped at a movie theater, and Ron and Joe asked if they could join them. Marilynn said, "It's a free country."

They sat together in the balcony and ate popcorn and watched the movie. Ron leaned close to Marilynn and asked for some popcorn. Not realizing how close he was, she hit his face with the box when she moved her arm, and the popcorn flew everywhere. She laughed uproariously. He suddenly liked her even more. It wasn't just sexual attraction, although there was plenty of that. He felt something he'd never quite experienced.

They left the movie theater and stopped at a coffee shop, where Ron and Marilynn split a piece of Boston cream pie with their coffee. The girls had to move along, but Ron had managed to find out that Marilynn was a file clerk at the navy yard, in Building 101.

Ron found her there the next day, and he made a spectacle of himself until she agreed to meet him for lunch. After that he began to see her almost every day. Before too long, he told her he loved her, and to his joyful surprise, she declared she loved him, too.

Soon enough, he got invited to her home. Her father, Bruce Callaway, was an engineer on a navy yard train, and Mrs. Callaway and Marilynn's younger brothers made Ron feel most welcome. One night when they were going out to dinner and dancing, all dressed up, Marilynn's father offered to let them use his car. They made love for the first time at the end of that evening, in the car.

There was tension in Marilynn's family, especially between her and her mother, since the family was about to move back to Salida, Colorado, where Marilynn had grown up. Marilynn wanted to go ahead early and stay with her aunt Mary in Pueblo, Colorado, but her parents worried about her.

Since the time had come for Ron to take his leave, and he was going home to Indiana, he agreed to accompany Marilynn on the train as far as Pueblo. But they got off the train at Ogden, Utah, and spent the night there in a hotel. The next day, as they continued on to Pueblo, Marilynn decided she wanted to stay in a hotel for one more night before arriving at her aunt's. She called her aunt's house from the hotel to tell her that she was in town and would arrive shortly, but her uncle answered the phone. He soon showed up at the hotel acting strangely. For some reason he picked that moment to tell Marilynn that Bruce Callaway, the man she had always known as her father, was in fact her stepfather. Marilynn was so upset by the revelation that she couldn't face going to stay with her aunt and uncle.

Ron called his father and asked him to wire enough money to buy a ticket for Marilynn to come to Hammond, Indiana, with him. Ron's family welcomed Marilynn into their home. But a week later, Ron found her in her room crying. She told him she was pregnant. He didn't want to get married yet. He had to go back to sea all too soon, and he didn't want a wife back home to worry about, and certainly not a wife and child. But it never occurred to him not to marry Marilynn. If you got a girl pregnant, you married her, plain and simple. That was the code he'd been taught.

On a bright, breezy afternoon on the twenty-fourth of May, Ron Smith and Marilynn Callaway were married by a Methodist minister on his family's front lawn with his parents, younger brother and sister, and a few other relatives looking on. Marilynn's pregnancy later turned out to be a false alarm, but the marriage was for real.

One of Ron's uncles owned a used-car lot, and he gave them a good deal on a red 1940 Chevy. They got in touch with one of Ron's shipmates and his wife, who agreed to drive back to California with them, which gave them enough rationed gas to get there. On the way, they stopped off in Colorado to see Marilynn's parents, who had completed their move to Salida.

Then it was on to California, where the navy gave them a Quonset hut to live in for thirty days. After that, Marilynn found a room in Vallejo. They sold the Chevy. Ron said the payments were too much to keep up with, but he also didn't want Marilynn tooling around in that conspicuous flaming-red car while he was away. He seriously doubted that a girl who liked sex as much as Marilynn did was going to be faithful while he was at sea, and he didn't want her to attract too much attention from other men.

The *Seal* went to sea again soon after D-Day, without Ron. He had been transferred to a new submarine that was under construction. Then, during a routine physical, the medics decided that he was suffering from combat fatigue and no longer fit for submarine duty.

Three months later, Ron was transferred to fleet torpedo school in Great Lakes, Illinois, as an instructor. Marilynn went with him, and they found a one-room rental in Kenosha, Wisconsin, from which Ron commuted every day to Great Lakes, except when he was on duty and couldn't leave the base.

Meanwhile, Marilynn got pregnant for real, and the day after Christmas 1944, she returned home to stay with her mother for the duration of the pregnancy, as was customary then for military wives.

They wrote letters regularly, but Ron still felt out of touch with his young, pregnant bride. They couldn't afford long-distance phone calls except in emergencies, so they almost never spoke. Ron did get one happy call, though. On May 17, 1945, his mother-in-law phoned to tell him he had a son. The couple decided to name him Ronal Lynn, a combination of both their names.

In June, Ron was transferred to the naval ammunition depot at Crane, Indiana, where Marilynn was supposed to join him as soon as she and the baby were strong enough to travel. Instead, she sent him a "Dear John" letter.

Marilynn declared that their marriage had been a mistake. Ron was not entirely surprised. When he was discharged in August, shortly after the war ended, he was free to do what he wanted with his life, if only he knew what that was. Truthfully, he had expected to die in the war, as so many submariners had. His father reminded him that he had a son to think about, and he should earn some money and go try to patch things up with Marilynn. Ron knew his father was right.

So he went to work loading boxcars and set off for Colorado in November in a 1936 Pontiac he bought for $350. He ran into a blizzard but kept going, even persuading the state police to let him pass a barricade. He reached Salida at midday and got a motel room. He then went to the Callaways' house.

When Marilynn answered the door, she was stunned to see him standing there. When she starting crying and threw her arms around him, he figured things would turn out all right. After several days of steady persuading, she agreed to get back together with him. He sold the Pontiac for twice what it had cost him. He planned to go to Houston, where he had a few relatives and had heard there were lots of jobs available. Once he'd landed one, he would send for Marilynn and his son. He gave her half the money from the Pontiac to save for her journey.

He soon found a job, but Marilynn never came. He wrote, but she never answered. Her parents intercepted his phone calls. He finally gave up when the operator told him their phone had been disconnected.

Ron finished high school while working in a greasy spoon, then went back to see his family in Indiana for the summer. He had intended to attend Texas A&M in the fall, but he met a girl named Georgianna and fell in love. He got a divorce from Marilynn in absentia and married Georgianna. They soon moved to Houston, where he settled into a career as a factory representative for automobile manufacturers.

He and Georgianna had five children. Ron made many attempts over the years to find Marilynn and, particularly, his son. But it seemed like they had dropped off the face of the earth.

In 1963, Ron was traveling for Checker Motors when he wandered into a small restaurant in Albuquerque, New Mexico, for dinner. The guy next to him struck up a conversation. He told Ron he had worked for the railroads most of his life. Offhandedly, Ron asked if he had ever known a Bruce Callaway—Marilynn's stepfather—who had been an engineer at the navy yards in San Francisco all those years ago. "Sure!" the man exclaimed. "Hell, I've known Bruce for years. Just saw him the other day."

Ron couldn't believe his ears. It turned out Bruce lived in Colorado City and was working for the Denver & Rio Grande Railroad. Ron quickly finished his dinner and went back to his room at the Ramada Inn. He called information and got Bruce Callaway's number in Colorado City. A man answered the phone.

"Is this Bruce Callaway?" Ron asked.

"Yes, who's this?"

"This is Ron—Ronnie Smith."

After a long pause, Bruce finally realized to whom he was speaking.

He explained to Ron that he and Marilynn's mother had divorced long ago. Marilynn's mother had married a retired army guy and was living with him in Chandler, Arizona. Marilynn, in turn, had married someone else and was living somewhere in Nevada. Ron asked if his son was with Marilynn.

"No," replied Bruce, "he's with his grandmother in Chandler."

Ron thanked Bruce for the information. After an awkward silence, Bruce added, "Ronnie, I'm real sorry about what happened, but it wasn't my fault." Ron told him that he understood, thanked him again, and hung up.

Ron knew better than to try to reach his son through his former mother-in-law. But he knew the boy would have to be in high school, so he got the number of the Chandler school and called there directly the very next morning. When a clerk answered, Ron said, "This is an emergency, I need to talk to my son Ronal Lynn Smith."

The clerk said, "Let's see, oh, he's in math class, hold on, I'll get him."

In a few minutes, a young man's voice came on the line. "Hello?"

"Hello to you, this is your father."

Both too emotional to make much sense, they managed to stumble through an exchange of home addresses and phone numbers.

Just a few weeks later, Ron went to Chandler for a weekend visit with his son. He took a room in Scottsdale, picked up Ronal Lynn, and they spent the weekend together trying to get acquainted. It was an awkward time, but a few months later, his son made a reciprocal visit to Dallas, where Ron now lived with his family.

They began to correspond by mail. Over the years, the contacts became less frequent, until Ronal Lynn got married himself. His wife, Jeanne, made an effort to write to Ron more often, and the two men began to exchange phone calls on a regular basis. It was, Ron felt, as good an outcome as could be expected, considering that he hadn't seen his son since Ronal was an infant. They could never make up for the missing years, but they ultimately developed a very worthwhile friendship.

Meanwhile, Ron had other problems to deal with. He had two heart attacks a week apart in 1980 and had to undergo open-heart surgery in June, involving five bypasses. Ron quit smoking and recovered with few complications.

Then, in 1982, he was laid off from his job as a fleet administrator for a major oil-service company that was in a downsizing cycle. He got a similar job with another company, which only lasted nine months before he was downsized out of work again. He and Georgianna were forced into a "friendly foreclosure" on the house they had lived in for the past ten years.

Ron launched his own business making consoles for pickups, a device he had designed himself. The same oil slump that had cost Ron his jobs hit his younger brother Rex, who owned a furniture business in Texas. They joined forces to manufacture and sell the consoles Ron had created, and the business flourished.

In the meantime, under the strain of Ron's illnesses and their financial hardships, Ron and Georgianna had grown apart. They slept in separate bedrooms. All of their children were by then on their own. Their youngest boy was still in college at Rice University, but they'd furnished him with enough financial support to fend for himself.

Ron felt weary with his life and decided he needed a break to rejuvenate himself. Georgianna encouraged this and even arranged his flight plans and car rental through the travel agency where she had been working for the past four years. Ron started off his journey by flying to Sacramento and driving up to Willows, California, to visit Ronal Lynn and Jeanne for a couple of weeks.

Over the years, Ron had learned the benefits of forgiveness, coming to understand that grudges always hurt the person holding them the most. So he asked Ronal Lynn to arrange for his mother, who now lived 120 miles to the north in Yreka, to come down to Willows for a visit. Ronal did so, and soon it was settled that Marilynn would drive there, arriving early Friday evening. By eight o'clock on Friday night, she still hadn't arrived. Ron began to worry that she had changed her mind. About eight-thirty, though, she finally rolled into the driveway. Ron stood on the porch steps as Ronal Lynn and Jeanne went out to greet her and help her with her bags.

Ron looked at her as she walked toward him. She was older—the wrinkles around her mouth attested to that—and a little wider in the hips, but she was still quite a beautiful woman at sixty.

"Is that really you?" Marilynn asked as she walked toward him, squinting and then shading her eyes with her hand.

"Yes, it's me," Ron said and smiled at her.

She put out her hands, and Ron took them in his. They looked at each other for a long moment and then, as if it had been rehearsed, drew closer and kissed each other on the cheek, like old friends. They walked into the living room, where Ron stopped and took her hands again. He had gone over the words he wanted to say to her so many times in his head, and now he was able to say them out loud. "I just want to tell you that I forgive you anything you have done to me, and ask that you forgive me anything that I might have done to you."

She looked dumbfounded, and tears began rolling down her cheeks. The she threw her arms around him, crying out, "Oh God, it's always been you." They kissed fully and tenderly on the mouth. He pushed her away gently and looked into her ice-blue eyes and said, "My God, I'm still in love with you." It seemed to him that at that moment they were completely alone in the universe.

They spent the rest of the weekend driving into the mountains, going out to dinner, talking all the time. She laughed at all his jokes, funny or not. They talked most of the night. He invited her into his room, saying, "You don't have to worry. I'll stay under the covers and you can stay on top of them." And that's exactly what they did.

Marilynn called and arranged to take Monday off from work, too, giving them another day together. They agreed that Ron would return to Texas, conclude his involvements there, and come to live with Marilynn in Yreka.

Ron flew home and told Georgianna that he was moving to California permanently; he turned the business over to his brother Rex. Ronal Lynn flew down to help his dad drive to California, and they met Jeanne and Marilynn in Reno, spending the weekend there. Ron and Marilynn made love most of the night, as if it were their second honeymoon.

Monday morning, Ronal Lynn and Jeanne drove off to Willows, and Ron and Marilynn headed for Yreka. She was renting a cottage nestled at the foot of Mount Shasta.

Aggravated by the smallness of the space, and complicated by their ties to other people, including their children, from the past they had not shared, Ron and Marilyn's relationship was tempestuous. But in spite of all that, and despite a promise Marilynn had once made to herself never to marry again, she agreed to marry Ron.

Ron made several trips back to Texas to visit his children and help Rex with the business. In November 1985, Georgianna agreed to a divorce that was quickly settled. Ron was now free to marry Marilynn, but she kept hesitating. At one point, they went to Reno, with Ronal Lynn and Jeanne in tow, and got a marriage license. But the next day Marilynn backed out. It reminded Ron of the old times.

Finally, in June 1987, Ron decided that he'd had enough. He packed all his things and went back to Texas to stay with his brother. Not only did Marilynn refuse to marry him, she had also lost interest in sex. Marilynn had started feeling unwell in February 1987. Ron had taken her to several doctors, but they could find nothing wrong.

While Ron was in Texas, Marilynn called, crying, and begged him to come back. He never had been able to handle her crying, so he agreed, provided that she at last marry him for real. They were married in Las Vegas that August. Briefly, she seemed to feel better physically, but then her symptoms worsened. Ron was convinced they were psychosomatic, tied up somehow with their relationship. But in September, a new doctor diagnosed Marilynn with scleroderma, a rare progressive disease that gradually causes a hardening of the skin. The doctor ordered additional tests, but they had to be sent to Stanford Medical Center for confirmation, which could take as long as three weeks.

Marilynn urged Ron to visit Texas in the meantime, and he did, visiting his brother and two of his sons. He also saw Georgianna and was happy to find that they got along like old friends.

Ron flew back to California on Friday the thirteenth, deliberately pushing aside his superstition. There he found Marilynn suffering more than ever, sleeping fitfully and going to the bathroom nearly once an hour. In the morning he fixed her a big breakfast, but she ate very little. She said she needed a new nightgown and asked him to buy her one. Dutifully, he went out and purchased the kind of "shortie" she liked. Ron tried to watch television the rest of the day while Marilynn slept. He told her he would make some potato soup for supper, which she thought sounded good, but again she couldn't, or wouldn't, eat much.

At nine o'clock, Ron lay down beside her, very tired but almost too tense and fearful to sleep. At eleven-thirty, she woke him, asking him to help her to the bathroom. He went around to her side of the bed and knelt in front of her to help her stand. She put her hand on top of his head and cried out, "Oh, Ronnie, I love you so much." Ron smiled up at her, but she started coughing and grabbed her throat. "I can't breathe," she choked out, and fell back on her side of the bed. Her eyes were open but looked strange and vacant.

Ron felt for a heartbeat, but there was none. "Don't leave me!" he screamed.

He tried to give her CPR, stopping to call 911, then starting again. The paramedics arrived, and Ron followed the ambulance to the hospital. He waited more than an hour. Finally a doctor came out, shaking his head. "I'm sorry, we tried everything to revive her, she's gone." But Ron already knew.

The doctor asked Ron if he needed a prescription to help him sleep. He declined and went back to the house and lay down. That night he had an extremely vivid dream. He saw a vision of Marilynn walking up a beautiful green slope. A figure in white held her hand, and a brilliant light shimmered in the background. Marilynn turned back to him and smiled. "It's okay, honey. I'm fine now. I love you."

Ron went back to Texas. After a time, he and Georgianna remarried, and he knew that he was back where he belonged. But he feels that his reunion with Marilynn, and the late, last years with her, was something preordained. Fate insisted he return to her and finish the love they had begun so many years before.

*Ron, torpedoman second class, home on leave in 1944.*

*Marilynn in front of the Vallejo, California, hotel where she and Ron lived, 1944.*

ANY WAR BRINGS SUFFERING, BUT *a global war creates truly unimaginable destruction. The death toll during World War II reached a staggering 50 million, an average of 192,307 dead for each week of the war. Yet some of those who survived don't see the war as an entirely destructive force. Many men and women who met and married in the course of World War II are acutely aware that if it had not been for the war, they never would have encountered each other. They mean no disrespect for the dead, nor do they make light in any way of the war's horrors; but there are those who feel that God was watching over them during the war, because the great conflict thrust them into each other's arms and lives. Because their lives together have meant so much, they cannot help but give thanks that the dire exigencies of war enabled them to find each other.*

*Kathleen and Raymond Withers*
*on their first date, July 5, 1942.*

# Raymond and Kathleen

## WITHERS

On July 4, 1942, Clara Kathleen Mitchell, just eighteen, attended her first USO dance in her hometown of Birmingham, Alabama. She and a girl-friend danced with a number of soldiers that night, many of them from Maxwell Field in Montgomery. One of the soldiers was Raymond Withers, a Kentucky farm boy who had joined the FBI, then enlisted in the army air corps in 1941. Four years older than Kathleen (as she preferred to be called), he was training as an aviation cadet at Maxwell Field, in hopes of becoming a pilot.

Kathleen spent that night at her friend's house. The next day, another cadet, who was a friend of Ray's, had arranged a date with Kathleen's friend. When he called, he asked her to bring Kathleen along for Ray. The date started off by attending services at the Methodist church in downtown Birmingham, then they all had lunch together and went out to the Birmingham airport to watch the planes taking off and landing.

The group was having such a good time that they dawdled a little too long, and Ray and his friend missed the last bus back to Montgomery and Maxwell Field, where they were due at six P.M. The two cadets resorted to thumbing a ride. To their surprise, before long, a limousine stopped for them. The man riding in back turned out to be the state highway com-missioner, and he ordered his driver "to get these boys back to Maxwell Field" on time. So the limousine took off down the highway at high speed—with no worries about being stopped by the police—and Ray and his friend were delivered in plenty of time.

Kathleen had made quite an impression on Ray that day, and when he returned to Birmingham a while later, he called her for a date that night, but she was already booked. Ray would not be so easily thwarted, however, and he started a correspondence with her, writing letters and sending her flowers. As Ray recalls, "This was less than a year after Pearl Harbor, and members of the local communities around the bases were extremely hospitable, generous, and anxious to entertain soldiers. I met many young ladies in those days, but not one of them affected me like Kathleen had on only one weekend."

As his training continued, Ray was first transferred from Maxwell Field to Greenville, Mississippi, for basic flight school, and then to Dothan, Alabama, for advanced training. He continued to write to Kathleen during those many months and persuaded her to come to Dothan on February 16, 1943, to attend the ceremony at which he received his wings and his commission as a second lieutenant. A few days later, on his way to Westover Field, in Massachusetts, Ray stopped off to see Kathleen in Birmingham, spending three days. Those few days convinced Ray that Kathleen was the one for him, and shortly thereafter, he wrote to his mother to tell her he had met the girl he was going to marry. "But he didn't tell me that," Kathleen remembers with a laugh.

Ray says when he danced with Kathleen on that first night, "There was a mystical feeling and attraction about her. This attraction has grown continually and will never leave me." In addition to the obvious chemistry between them, Ray says she had a "physical pull on my heart."

Aside from their attraction, Ray believes other more practical factors also brought them together. "We were both from lower-middle-class rural areas—Kathleen's parents were from Alabama farm families, and my family was Kentucky farmers. We both knew about the sacrifices necessary to live a Christian life and to be proud of our heritage and country. Both of our families had hit bottom during the Depression, when we were children. Kathleen's father had lost his drugstore and had to start over doing various jobs. Until 1930 my father was a very successful tobacco farmer, but the Depression broke him both financially and physically. He lost his farm and had to start over on a small and less productive one. He never really recovered and died in 1938 at the age of sixty-four. We lived without electricity until 1936 and had never had indoor plumbing."

Both Ray and Kathleen worked all through high school, but despite their good grades, college proved too much of a financial hardship. Kathleen was granted a small scholarship, but it didn't cover enough of the expenses for college. Ray had saved enough money for three semesters at the University of Kentucky during 1938–39, but he eventually had to drop out to earn more money. He went from job to job, in addition to helping his mother and brother run the small family farm.

Ray took every possible civil service exam until he finally got a job as a fingerprint classifier at the FBI in Washington, D.C. He started there on February 23, 1941, and volunteered for the army air corps ten months later on December 9, two days after Pearl Harbor was bombed. That's when he was sent to Maxwell Field for training, where he arrived in March 1942. Kathleen, who had already had one post–high school job with Sears, Roebuck, was by then working for Tennessee Coal and Iron.

Through all the letter writing, and with all of this common experience, they developed a remarkable understanding, even though Ray's visit to Birmingham was just the third time they'd seen each other in six months. After Ray's visit to Birmingham, they didn't see each other again until Ray had flown a full tour of seventy-two missions as a P-47 pilot in the Eighth Air Force in England.

They continued to write letters back and forth. Kathleen sent Ray care packages, and he sent her flowers, gifts, and poems. Kathleen believes that these letters allowed them to get to know each other very deeply. "During the war," she says, "people had a tendency to know what was important and were able to express themselves more than we do today."

At the end of his first tour, Ray could either sign up for another tour, after a thirty-day leave back in the States, or he could choose assignment to noncombat duty in England with no leave. He felt he could not pass up a chance to see Kathleen, so he chose a second tour and arrived in New York for his leave on July 12, 1944. First he went to Kentucky to see his mother and brother, then hastened to Birmingham to visit Kathleen, arriving on July 24. This would be only the fourth time they had seen each other in the nearly two years since their dance at the USO.

That Monday night, Ray asked Kathleen to marry him. Although she considered herself quite mature for her twenty years, she wasn't sure she was ready to get married. Her first response was to suggest that it would be nice "just to be engaged" for a while. But Ray insisted that it was marriage or nothing. "I'm not going to go back overseas and get a Dear John letter," he told her.

On Wednesday, she still hadn't given him a definite answer. Then, walking in downtown Birmingham, they stopped at a corner to wait for the light to change. At that moment, something came together in Kathleen's head. "All right," she suddenly blurted out, "I will marry you." Ray looked at her in astonishment. "Well, this is a fine place to tell me, waiting for a light to change!"

They went across the street to a drugstore and sat down to talk over a Coke. First, they realized, they had to get blood tests. As they came out of the drugstore, Kathleen looked up and realized that the office of her father's doctor was in the building right in front of them. They went in and explained to the receptionist that they needed blood tests, and were told to sit in the waiting room, which was full of pregnant women. After just a few minutes, they were ushered into the office of a doctor, who turned out to be the brother of the doctor they were looking for, but he was happy to help them. He looked them over and told Kathleen that he knew she was a splendid young woman, and Ray was clearly a fine young man bravely serving his country. So they didn't have to bother with the blood test. He'd just sign the papers. With that taken care of, they went over to city hall to apply for the license and were told they could pick it up the very next day.

That night, Kathleen's father had plans to take them out to dinner. They needed his permission to marry, because Kathleen was under twenty-one. But Ray wouldn't bring up the subject while they were eating. Kathleen finally went to the ladies' room to leave the two men alone. When Ray asked her father's permission to take Kathleen's hand, her father readily granted it. But Ray has never forgotten the two things he said. First he looked keenly at Ray and said, "I'm losing a daughter, not gaining a son." He also offered his prospective son-in-law a piece of advice: "Never go to sleep angry at each other." In essence, Ray knows, he was "letting me know that I was now responsible for her."

On Thursday, Ray and Kathleen made the rest of their wedding arrangements. The ceremony took place at seven o'clock the Friday night after the Monday that Ray had proposed.

In a book of letters compiled for Ray by friends and family in honor of his eightieth birthday in August 1999, Kathleen wrote, "Our wedding day, with you, Daddy and Brother Astin the only men there—because everyone else was overseas—July 28, 1944, will always have such a special place among all my memories because that was the start of a wonderful life for me. Our honeymoon in Gatlinburg, Tennessee—swimming in the creek and then back to the room!!! Those wonderful meals in a place far removed from the worry of the war. The trip on the train to your hometown—meeting family and friends I had never met before, and that last night in Cincinnati, when we thought you were going overseas and we wouldn't see one another until after another tour of missions."

After their brief honeymoon, Kathleen returned to Birmingham and her job at Tennessee Coal and Iron, and Ray headed back east, expecting to ship out for England right away. But not long after, Ray called to tell Kathleen that he had been given the opportunity to spend a few days of R&R at a hotel in Atlantic City. She had to quit her job to go and meet him, but she didn't hesitate to catch the train north. This was only her second time on a train, and her first trip alone. "There was no air-conditioning in those days, of course," Kathleen notes, "and I was a sight when I got off the train in Atlantic City."

Ray had been staying since August 18 at the Ritz-Carlton Hotel, which the military had taken over as an R&R retreat. When Kathleen arrived on the twenty-first, they had no rooms for couples available, so in order to be together, she and Ray spent four nights at the Chelsea Hotel at $10 a night. For the following eight days, though, they were given a private room at the posh Ritz-Carlton, and they reveled in the luxury. Ray's total bill at the Ritz for seventeen days was $16.75. "That fantastic room for only pennies," Kathleen wrote in Ray's eightieth birthday letter, "and the walks on the boardwalk."

Kathleen endured a lonely trip back to Birmingham, where she soon got a new job with the government, operating calculating machines. Ray flew another full tour of missions, earning many medals, including a Silver Star, and finally returning to Birmingham on March 25, 1945.

Ray remained in the military even after the war. Their first child, their daughter Carol, was born December 20, 1945, in Fort Leavenworth, Kansas, where Ray was stationed at Sherman Field.

Ray and his crew with his P-47, with Kathleen's name painted on its nose.

The hut built by crew chief Tony Librandi, with Kathleen Ann flag flying.

Ray back in England for his second tour, sitting on the wing of his P-51.

*Ray and Kathleen on their wedding day, July 28, 1944.*

*Ray and Kathleen at his retirement party in 1972.*

*Ray and Kathleen at home on their fifty-sixth wedding anniversary, July 28, 2000.*

Over the years, Ray more than compensated for his initially truncated time at the University of Kentucky, earning a BEE from Ohio State University in 1949 and an MBA from the University of Chicago in 1953. He also studied Japanese for a year at Yale University before being posted to Japan from 1957 to 1960.

By that time, Kathleen decided that he'd had enough education, since every time he went back to school they had another child—four in all. They now have eleven grandchildren and three great-grandchildren and have been "having a ball" since Ray's retirement as a colonel in 1972.

Looking back on their fifty-seven happy years of marriage, Kathleen is gratified that she didn't listen to the people who were convinced that the two of them couldn't possibly have gotten to know each other well enough in the tiny amount of time they spent together before their wedding. For his part, Ray maintains, "I'm firmly convinced that God had a hand in my decision on July 4, 1942, to take a bus a hundred miles to Birmingham instead of going two miles into Montgomery after being confined to post for over two months."